Electronic Crime Scene Investigation: A Guide for First Responders

The Internet, computer networks, and automated data systems present an enormous new opportunity for committing criminal activity. Computers and other electronic devices are being used increasingly to commit, enable, or support crimes perpetrated against persons, organizations, or property. Whether the crime involves attacks against computer systems, the information they contain, or more traditional crimes such as murder, money laundering, trafficking, or fraud, electronic evidence increasingly is involved. It is no surprise that law enforcement and criminal justice officials are being overwhelmed by the volume of investigations and prosecutions that involve electronic evidence. This book was released by the U.S. Department of Justice in July 2001.

Why buy a book you can download for free? We print this book so you don't have to.

Some books are only available on line, so you gotta print your own if you want hard copy (paper). You could print it using a network printer you share with 100 other people (typically the network printer is jammed, its out of paper or out of toner). If it's just a 10-page document, no problem, but if it's a large document, you will need to punch 3 holes in all those pages and put them in a 3-ring binder. Takes at least an hour.

It's much more cost-effective to just order the latest version from Amazon.com

This book includes original artwork and commentary which is the only copyright material. Note that government documents are in the public domain. We print these large documents as a service so you don't have to.

Other books we print on Amazon.com:

Prosecuting Intellectual Property Crimes
Prosecuting Computer Crimes
Criminal Resource Manual (CRM) 2019
Civil Resource Manual (2019)
Justice Manual (JM) 2019
Treasury Antitrust Division Manual (2017)
Rules of the Supreme Court of the United States (Effective November 13, 2017)
Naval Legal Service Command Manual (2013)
Budget of the United States Government, Fiscal Year 2020
Federal Rules of Appellate Procedure (2017)
Federal Rules of Criminal Procedure (2017)
Federal Rules of Civil Procedure (2017)
Federal Rules of Bankruptcy Procedure (2017)
Benchbook for U.S. District Court Judges (2013)
Military Judges' Benchbook (2017)
Principles of Federal Appropriations Law 4th Edition
Immigration Court Practice Manual
DoD Law of War Manual (2016)
DoD Operational Law Handbook (2017)
DoD Domestic Operational Law Handbook (2015 DOPLAW)
DoD Rule of Law Handbook (2015)
Uniform Code of Military Justice (2018)
Manual for Courts-Martial (2019)
DoD Commander's Legal Handbook (2015)
The Military Commander and the Law (2017)
U.S. Courts Design Guide + Standard Level Features and Finishes
GAO Government Auditing Standards 2018 Final (Yellow Book)
GAO Standards for Internal Control in the Federal Government (Green Book)
United States Sentencing Commission Guidelines Manual
U.S. Senate Manual
Rules of the House of Representatives
U.S. House Practice
Criminal Law Deskbook
Law of Federal Employment
Fiscal Law Deskbook
Contract Attorneys Deskbook

Visit usgovpub.com

Electronic Crime Scene Investigation: A Guide for First Responders

Written and Approved by the Technical Working Group for Electronic Crime Scene Investigation

July 2001

U.S. Department of Justice
Office of Justice Programs
National Institute of Justice

This document is not intended to create, does not create, and may not be relied upon to create any rights, substantive or procedural, enforceable at law by any party in any matter civil or criminal.

Opinions or points of view expressed in this document represent a consensus of the authors and do not necessarily represent the official position or policies of the U.S. Department of Justice. The products and manufacturers discussed in this document are presented for informational purposes only and do not constitute product approval or endorsement by the U.S. Department of Justice.

NCJ 187736

The National Institute of Justice is a component of the Office of Justice Programs, which also includes the Bureau of Justice Assistance, the Bureau of Justice Statistics, the Office of Juvenile Justice and Delinquency Prevention, and the Office for Victims of Crime.

Forward

The Internet, computer networks, and automated data systems present an enormous new opportunity for committing criminal activity. Computers and other electronic devices are being used increasingly to commit, enable, or support crimes perpetrated against persons, organizations, or property. Whether the crime involves attacks against computer systems, the information they contain, or more traditional crimes such as murder, money laundering, trafficking, or fraud, electronic evidence increasingly is involved. It is no surprise that law enforcement and criminal justice officials are being overwhelmed by the volume of investigations and prosecutions that involve electronic evidence.

To assist State and local law enforcement agencies and prosecutorial offices with the growing volume of electronic crime, a series of reference guides regarding practices, procedures, and decisionmaking processes for investigating electronic crime is being prepared by technical working groups of practitioners and subject matter experts who are knowledgeable about electronic crime. The practitioners and experts are from Federal, State, and local law enforcement agencies; criminal justice agencies; offices of prosecutors and district attorneys general; and academic, commercial, and professional organizations.

The series of guides will address the investigation process from the crime scene first responder, to the laboratory, to the courtroom. Specifically, the series of guides will address:

Crime scene investigations by first responders.

Examination of digital evidence.

Investigative uses of technology.

Investigating electronic technology crimes.

Creating a digital evidence forensic unit.

Courtroom presentation of digital evidence.

Due to the rapidly changing nature of electronic and computer technologies and of electronic crime, efforts will be periodically undertaken to update the information contained within each of the guides. The guides, and any subsequent updates that are made to them, will be made available on the National Institute of Justice's World Wide Web site (http://www.ojp.usdoj.gov/nij).

Technical Working Group for Electronic Crime Scene Investigation

The Technical Working Group for Electronic Crime Scene Investigation (TWGECSI) was a multidisciplinary group of practitioners and subject matter experts from across the United States and other nations. Each of the individual participants is experienced in the intricacies involved with electronic evidence in relation to recognition, documentation, collection, and packaging. To initiate the working group, a planning panel composed of a limited number of participants was selected to define the scope and breadth of the work. A series of guides was proposed in which each guide will focus on a different aspect of the discipline.

The panel chose crime scene investigation as the first topic for incorporation into a guide.

Planning Panel

Susan Ballou
Program Manager for Forensic
    Sciences
Office of Law Enforcement Standards
National Institute of Standards and
    Technology
Gaithersburg, Maryland

Jaime Carazo
Special Agent
United States Secret Service
Electronic Crimes Branch
Washington, D.C.

Bill Crane
Assistant Director
Computer Crime Section
National White Collar Crime Center
Fairmont, West Virginia

Fred Demma
National Law Enforcement and
    Corrections Technology
    Center–Northeast
Rome, New York

Grant Gottfried
Special Projects
National Center for Forensic Science
Orlando, Florida

Sam Guttman
Assistant Inspector in Charge
Forensic and Technical Services
U.S. Postal Inspection Service
Dulles, Virginia

Jeffrey Herig
Special Agent
Florida Department of Law
    Enforcement
Florida Computer Crime Center
Tallahassee, Florida

Tim Hutchison
Sheriff
Knox County Sheriff's Office
Knoxville, Tennessee

David Icove
Manager, Special Projects
U.S. TVA Police
Knoxville, Tennessee

Bob Jarzen
Sacramento County
Laboratory of Forensic Science
Sacramento, California

Tom Johnson
Dean
School of Public Safety and
  Professional Studies
University of New Haven
West Haven, Connecticut

Karen Matthews
DOE Computer Forensic Laboratory
Bolling AFB
Washington, D.C.

Mark Pollitt
Unit Chief
FBI–CART
Washington, D.C.

David Poole
Director
DoD Computer Forensics Laboratory
Linthicum, Maryland

Mary Riley
Price Waterhouse Coopers, LLP
Washington, D.C.

Kurt Schmid
Director
National HIDTA Program
Washington, D.C.

Howard A. Schmidt
Corporate Security Officer
Microsoft Corp.
Redmond, Washington

Raemarie Schmidt
Computer Crime Specialist
National White Collar Crime Center
Computer Crime Section
Fairmont, West Virginia

Carl Selavka
Massachusetts State Police Crime
  Laboratory
Sudbury, Massachusetts

Steve Sepulveda
United States Secret Service
Washington, D.C.

Todd Shipley
Detective Sergeant
Reno Police Department
Financial/Computer Crimes Unit
Reno, Nevada

Chris Stippich
Computer Crime Specialist
Computer Crime Section
National White Collar Crime Center
Fairmont, West Virginia

Carrie Morgan Whitcomb
Director
National Center for Forensic Science
Orlando, Florida

Wayne Williams
Sr. Litigation Counsel
Computer Crime and Intellectual
  Property Section
Criminal Division
U.S. Department of Justice
Washington, D.C.

TWGECSI Members

Additional members were then incorporated into TWGECSI to provide a full technical working group. The individuals listed below, along with those participants on the planning panel, worked together to produce this guide for electronic crime scene first responders.

Abigail Abraham
Assistant State's Attorney
Cook County State's Attorney's Office
Chicago, Illinois

Keith Ackerman
Head of CID
Police HQ
Hampshire Constabulary
Winchester, Hants
United Kingdom

Michael Anderson
President
New Technologies, Inc
Gresham, Oregon

Bill Baugh
CEO
Savannah Technology Group
Savannah, Georgia

Randy Bishop
Special Agent in Charge
U.S. Department of Energy
Office of Inspector General
Technology Crime Section
Washington, D.C.

Steve Branigan
Vice President of Product
    Development
Lucent Technologies
Murray Hill, New Jersey

Paul Brown
CyberEvidence, Inc.
The Woodlands, Texas

Carleton Bryant
Staff Attorney
Knox County Sheriff's Office
Knoxville, Tennessee

Christopher Bubb
Deputy Attorney General
New Jersey Division of Criminal
    Justice
Trenton, New Jersey

Don Buchwald
Project Engineer
National Law Enforcement and
    Corrections Technology
    Center–West
The Aerospace Corporation
Los Angeles, California

Cheri Carr
Computer Forensic Lab Chief
NASA Office of the Inspector General
Network and Advanced Technology
    Protections Office
Washington, D.C.

Nick Cartwright
Manager
Canadian Police Research Centre
Ottawa, Ontario
Canada

Ken Citarella
Chief
High Tech Crimes Bureau
Westchester County District Attorney
White Plains, New York

Chuck Coe
Director of Technical Services
NASA Office of the Inspector General
Network and Advanced Technology
    Protections Office
Washington, D.C.

Fred Cohen
Sandia National Laboratories
Cyber Defender Program
Livermore, California

Fred Cotton
Director of Training Services
SEARCH
The National Consortium for Justice
    Information and Statistics
Sacramento, California

Tony Crisp
Lieutenant
Maryville Police Department
Maryville, Tennessee

Mark Dale
New York State Police
Forensic Investigation Center
Albany, New York

Claude Davenport
Senior SA
United States Customs Service
Sterling, Virginia

David Davies
Photographic Examiner
Federal Bureau of Investigation
Washington, D.C.

Michael Donhauser
Maryland State Police
Columbia, Maryland

James Doyle
Sergeant
Detective Bureau
New York City Police Department
New York, New York

Michael Duncan
Sergeant
Royal Canadian Mounted Police
Economic Crime Branch
Technological Crime Section
Ottawa, Ontario
Canada

Jim Dunne
Group Supervisor
Drug Enforcement Agency
St. Louis, Missouri

Chris Duque
Detective
Honolulu Police Department
White Collar Crime Unit
Honolulu, Hawaii

Doug Elrick
Iowa DCI Crime Lab
Des Moines, Iowa

Paul French
Computer Forensics Lab Manager
New Technologies Armor, Inc.
Gresham, Oregon

Gerald Friesen
Electronic Search Coordinator
Industry Canada
Hull, Quebec
Canada

Pat Gilmore, CISSP
Director
Information Security
Atomic Tangerine
San Francisco, California

Gary Gordon
Professor
Economic Crime Programs
Utica College
WetStone Technologies
Utica, New York

Dan Henry
Chief Deputy
Marion County Sheriff's Department
Ocala, Florida

Jeff Hormann
Special Agent In Charge
Computer Crime Resident Agency
U.S. Army CID
Ft. Belvoir, Virginia

Mary Horvath
Program Manager
FBI–CART
Washington, D.C.

Mel Joiner
Officer
Arizona Department of Public Safety
Phoenix, Arizona

Nigel Jones
Detective Sergeant
Computer Crime Unit
Police Headquarters
Kent County Constabulary
Maidstone, Kent
United Kingdom

Jamie Kerr
SGT/Project Manager
RCMP Headquarters
Training Directorate
Ottawa, Ontario
Canada

Alan Kestner
Assistant Attorney General
Wisconsin Department of Justice
Madison, Wisconsin

Phil Kiracofe
Sergeant
Tallahassee Police Department
Tallahassee, Florida

Roland Lascola
Program Manager
FBI-CART
Washington, D.C.

Barry Leese
Detective Sergeant
Maryland State Police
Computer Crimes Unit
Columbia, Maryland

Glenn Lewis
Computer Specialist
SEARCH
The National Consortium for Justice
    Information and Statistics
Sacramento, California

Chris Malinowski
Forensic Computer Investigation
University of New Haven
West Haven, Connecticut

Kevin Manson
Director
Cybercop.org
St. Simons Island, Georgia

Brenda Maples
Lieutenant
Memphis Police Department
Memphis, Tennessee

Tim McAuliffe
New York State Police
Forensic Investigation Center
Albany, New York

Michael McCartney
Investigator
New York State Attorney General's
    Office
Criminal Prosecution Bureau–
    Organized Crime Task Force
Buffalo, New York

Alan McDonald
SSA
Washington, D.C.

Mark Menz
SEARCH
The National Consortium for Justice
    Information and Statistics
Sacramento, California

Dave Merkel
AOL Investigations
Reston, Virginia

Bill Moylan
Detective
Nassau County PD
Computer Crime Section
Crimes Against Property Squad
Westbury, New York

Steve Nesbitt
Director of Operations
NASA Office of the Inspector General
Network and Advanced Technology
  Protections Office
Washington, D.C.

Glen Nick
Program Manager
U.S. Customs Service
Cyber Smuggling Center
Fairfax, Virginia

Robert O'Leary
Detective
New Jersey State Police
High Technology Crimes &
  Investigations Support Unit
West Trenton, New Jersey

Matt Parsons
Special Agent/Division Chief
Naval Criminal Investigative Service
Washington, D.C.

Mike Phelan
Chief
Computer Forensics Unit
DEA Special Testing and Research
  Lab
Lorton, Virginia

Henry R. Reeve
General Counsel/Deputy D.A.
Denver District Attorney's Office
Denver, Colorado

Jim Riccardi, Jr.
Electronic Crime Specialist
National Law Enforcement and
  Corrections Technology
  Center–Northeast
Rome, New York

David Roberts
Deputy Executive Director
SEARCH
The National Consortium for Justice
  Information and Statistics
Sacramento, California

Leslie Russell
Forensic Science Service
Lambeth
London, England
United Kingdom

Greg Schmidt
Sr. Investigator
EDS-Investigations/Technical
Plano, Texas

George Sidor
Law Enforcement Security Consultant
Jaws Technologies Inc.
St. Albert, Alberta
Canada

William Spernow
CISSP
Research Director
Information Security Strategies Group
Gartner, Inc.
Suwanee, Georgia

Ronald Stevens
Senior Investigator
New York State Police
Forensic Investigation Center
Albany, New York

Gail Thackeray
Special Counsel–Technology Crimes
Arizona Attorney General's Office
Phoenix, Arizona

Dwight Van de Vate
Chief Deputy
Knox County Sheriff's Office
Knoxville, Tennessee

Jay Verhorevoort
Lieutenant
Davenport Police Department
Davenport, Iowa

Richard Vorder Bruegge
Photographic Examiner
Federal Bureau of Investigation
Washington, D.C.

Robert B. Wallace
U.S. Department of Energy
Germantown, Maryland

Craig Wilson
Detective Sergeant
Computer Crime Unit
Police Headquarters
Kent County Constabulary
Maidstone, Kent
United Kingdom

Brian Zwit
Chief Counsel (former)
Environment, Science, and Technology
National Association of Attorneys
  General
Washington, D.C.

Chronology

In May 1998, the National Cybercrime Training Partnership (NCTP), the Office of Law Enforcement Standards (OLES), and the National Institute of Justice (NIJ) collaborated on possible resources that could be implemented to counter electronic crime. Continuing meetings generated a desire to formulate one set of protocols that would address the process of electronic evidence from the crime scene through court presentations. NIJ selected the technical working group process as the way to achieve this goal but with the intent to create a publication flexible enough to allow implementation with any State and local law enforcement policy. Using its "template for technical working groups," NIJ established the Technical Working Group for Electronic Crime Scene Investigation (TWGECSI) to identify, define, and establish basic criteria to assist agencies with electronic investigations and prosecutions.

In January 1999, planning panel members met at the National Institute of Standards and Technology (NIST) in Gaithersburg, Maryland, to review the fast-paced arena of electronic crime and prepare the scope, intent, and objectives of the project. During this meeting, the scope was determined to be too vast for incorporation into one guide. Thus evolved a plan for several guides, each targeting separate issues. Crime scene investigation was selected as the topic for the first guide.

The initial meeting of the full TWGECSI took place March 1999 at NIST. After outlining tasks in a general meeting, the group separated into subgroups to draft the context of the chapters as identified by the planning panel. These chapters were Electronic Devices: Types and Potential Evidence; Investigative Tools and Equipment; Securing and Evaluating the Scene; Documenting the Scene; Evidence Collection; Packaging, Transportation, and Storage; and Forensic Examination by Crime Category. The volume of work involved in preparing the text of these chapters required additional TWGECSI meetings.

The planning panel did not convene again until May 2000. Due to the amount of time that had transpired between meetings, the planning panel reviewed the draft content and compared it with changes that had occurred in the electronic crime environment.

These revisions to the draft were then sent to the full TWGECSI in anticipation of the next meeting. The full TWGECSI met again at NIST in August 2000, and through 2 days of intense discussion, edited most of the draft to represent the current status of electronic crime investigation. With a few more sections requiring attention, the planning panel met in Seattle, Washington, during September 2000 to continue the editing process. These final changes, the glossary, and appendixes were then critiqued and voted on by the whole TWGECSI during the final meeting in November 2000 at NIST.

The final draft was then sent for content and editorial review to more than 80 organizations having expertise and knowledge in the electronic crime environment. The returned comments were evaluated and incorporated into the document when possible. The first chapter, Electronic Devices: Types and Potential Evidence, incorporates photographic representations of highlighted terms as a visual associative guide. At the end of the document are appendixes containing a glossary, legal resources, technical resources, training resources, and references, followed by a list of the organizations to which a draft copy of the document was sent.

Ackowledgments

The National Institute of Justice (NIJ) wishes to thank the members of the Technical Working Group for Electronic Crime Scene Investigation (TWGECSI) for their tireless dedication. There was a constant turnover of individuals involved, mainly as a result of job commitments and career changes. This dynamic environment resulted in a total of 94 individuals supplying their knowledge and expertise to the creation of the guide. All participants were keenly aware of the constant changes occurring in the field of electronics and strove to update information during each respective meeting. This demonstrated the strong desire of the working group to produce a guide that could be flexible and serve as a backbone for future efforts to upgrade the guide. In addition, NIJ offers a sincere thank you to each agency and organization represented by the working group members. The work loss to each agency during the absence of key personnel is evidence of management's commitment and understanding of the importance of standardization in forensic science.

NIJ also wishes to thank Kathleen Higgins, Director, and Susan Ballou, Program Manager, of the Office of Law Enforcement Standards, for providing management and guidance in bringing the project to completion.

NIJ would like to express appreciation for the input and support that Dr. David G. Boyd, Director of NIJ's Office of Science and Technology (OS&T), and Trent DePersia, Dr. Ray Downs, Dr. Richard Rau, Saralyn Borrowman, Amon Young, and James McNeil, all of OS&T, gave the meetings and the document. A special thanks is extended to Aspen Systems Corporation, specifically to Michele Coppola, the assigned editor, for her patience and skill in dealing with instantaneous transcription.

In addition, NIJ wishes to thank the law enforcement agencies, academic institutions, and commercial organizations worldwide that supplied contact information, reference materials, and editorial suggestions. Particular thanks goes to Michael R. Anderson, President of New Technologies, Inc., for contacting agencies knowledgeable in electronic evidence for inclusion in the appendix on technical resources.

Contents

Computers and other electronic devices are present in every aspect of modern life. At one time, a single computer filled an entire room; today, a computer can fit in the palm of your hand. The same technological advances that have helped law enforcement are being exploited by criminals.

Computers can be used to commit crime, can contain evidence of crime, and can even be targets of crime. Understanding the role and nature of electronic evidence that might be found, how to process a crime scene containing potential electronic evidence, and how an agency might respond to such situations are crucial issues. This guide represents the collected experience of the law enforcement community, academia, and the private sector in the recognition, collection, and preservation of electronic evidence in a variety of crime scenes.

The Law Enforcement Response to Electronic Evidence

The law enforcement response to electronic evidence requires that officers, investigators, forensic examiners, and managers all play a role. This document serves as a guide for the first responder. A first responder may be responsible for the recognition, collection, preservation, transportation, and/or storage of electronic evidence. In today's world, this can include almost everyone in the law enforcement profession. Officers may encounter electronic devices during their day-to-day duties. Investigators may direct the collection of electronic evidence, or may perform the collection themselves. Forensic examiners may provide assistance at crime scenes and will perform examinations on the evidence. Managers have the responsibility of ensuring that personnel under their direction are adequately trained and equipped to properly handle electronic evidence.

Each responder must understand the fragile nature of electronic evidence and the principles and procedures associated with its collection and preservation. Actions that have the potential to alter, damage, or destroy original evidence may be closely scrutinized by the courts.

Procedures should be in effect that promote electronic crime scene investigation. Managers should determine who will provide particular levels of services and how these services will be funded. Personnel should be provided with initial and ongoing technical training. Oftentimes, certain cases will demand a higher level of expertise, training, or equipment, and managers should have a plan in place regarding how to respond to these cases. The demand for responses to electronic evidence is expected to increase for the foreseeable future. Such services require that dedicated resources be allocated for these purposes.

The Latent Nature of Electronic Evidence

Electronic evidence is information and data of investigative value that is stored on or transmitted by an electronic device. As such, electronic evidence is latent evidence in the same sense that fingerprints or DNA (deoxyribonucleic acid) evidence are latent. In its natural state, we cannot "see" what is contained in the physical object that holds our evidence. Equipment and software are required to make the evidence visible. Testimony may be required to explain the examination process and any process limitations.

Electronic evidence is, by its very nature, fragile. It can be altered, damaged, or destroyed by improper handling or improper examination. For this reason, special precautions should be taken to document, collect, preserve, and examine this type of evidence. Failure to do so may render it unusable or lead to an inaccurate conclusion. This guide suggests methods that will help preserve the integrity of such evidence.

The Forensic Process

The nature of electronic evidence is such that it poses special challenges for its admissibility in court. To meet these challenges, follow proper forensic procedures. These procedures include, but are not limited to, four phases: collection, examination, analysis, and reporting. Although this guide concentrates on the collection phase, the nature of the other three phases and what happens in each are also important to understand.

The collection phase involves the search for, recognition of, collection of, and documentation of electronic evidence. The collection phase can involve real-time and stored information that may be lost unless precautions are taken at the scene.

The examination process helps to make the evidence visible and explain its origin and significance. This process should accomplish several things. First, it should document the content and state of the evidence in its totality. Such documentation allows all parties to discover what is contained in the evidence. Included in this process is the search for information that may be hidden or obscured. Once all the information is visible, the process of data reduction can begin, thereby separating the "wheat" from the "chaff." Given the tremendous amount of information that can be stored on computer storage media, this part of the examination is critical.

Analysis differs from examination in that it looks at the product of the examination for its significance and probative value to the case. Examination is a technical review that is the province of the forensic practitioner, while analysis is performed by the investigative team. In some agencies, the same person or group will perform both these roles.

A written report that outlines the examination process and the pertinent data recovered completes an examination. Examination notes must be preserved for discovery or testimony purposes. An examiner may need to testify about not only the conduct of the examination but also the validity of the procedure and his or her qualifications to conduct the examination.

This guide is intended for use by law enforcement and other responders who have the responsibility for protecting an electronic crime scene and for the recognition, collection, and preservation of electronic evidence. It is not all-inclusive. Rather, it deals with the most common situations encountered with electronic evidence. Technology is advancing at such a rapid rate that the suggestions in this guide must be examined through the prism of current technology and the practices adjusted as appropriate. It is recognized that all crime scenes are unique and the judgment of the first responder/investigator should be given deference in the implementation of this guide. Furthermore, those responsible officers or support personnel with special training should also adjust their practices as the circumstances (including their level of experience, conditions, and available equipment) warrant. This publication is not intended to address forensic analysis. Circumstances of individual cases and Federal, State, and local laws/rules may require actions other than those described in this guide.

When dealing with electronic evidence, general forensic and procedural principles should be applied:

Actions taken to secure and collect electronic evidence should not change that evidence.

Persons conducting examination of electronic evidence should be trained for the purpose.

Activity relating to the seizure, examination, storage, or transfer of electronic evidence should be fully documented, preserved, and available for review.

Who Is the Intended Audience for This Guide?

Anyone encountering a crime scene that might contain electronic evidence.

Anyone processing a crime scene that involves electronic evidence.

Anyone supervising someone who processes such a crime scene.

Anyone managing an organization that processes such a crime scene.

4

Without having the necessary skills and training, no responder should attempt to explore the contents or recover data from a computer (e.g., do not touch the keyboard or click the mouse) or other electronic device other than to record what is visible on its display.

What Is Electronic Evidence?

Electronic evidence is information and data of investigative value that is stored on or transmitted by an electronic device. Such evidence is acquired when data or physical items are collected and stored for examination purposes.

Electronic evidence:

Is often latent in the same sense as fingerprints or DNA evidence.

Can transcend borders with ease and speed.

Is fragile and can be easily altered, damaged, or destroyed.

Is sometimes time-sensitive.

How Is Electronic Evidence Handled at the Crime Scene?

Precautions must be taken in the collection, preservation, and examination of electronic evidence.

Handling electronic evidence at the crime scene normally consists of the following steps:

Recognition and identification of the evidence.

Documentation of the crime scene.

Collection and preservation of the evidence.

Packaging and transportation of the evidence.

The information in this document assumes that:

The necessary legal authority to search for and seize the suspected evidence has been obtained.

The crime scene has been secured and documented (photographically and/or by sketch or notes).

Crime scene protective equipment (gloves, etc.) is being used as necessary.

Note: First responders should use caution when seizing electronic devices. The improper access of data stored in electronic devices may violate provisions of certain Federal laws, including the Electronic Communications Privacy Act. Additional legal process may be necessary. Please consult your local prosecutor before accessing stored data on a device. Because of the fragile nature of electronic evidence, examination should be done by appropriate personnel.

Is Your Agency Prepared to Handle Electronic Evidence?

This document recommends that every agency identify local computer experts before they are needed. These experts should be "on call" for situations that are beyond the technical expertise of the first responder or department. (Similar services are in place for toxic waste emergencies.) It is also recommended that investigative plans be developed in compliance with departmental policy and Federal, State, and local laws. In particular, under the Privacy Protection Act, with certain exceptions, it is unlawful for an agent to search for or seize certain materials possessed by a person reasonably believed to have a purpose of disseminating information to the public. For example, seizure of First Amendment materials such as drafts of newsletters or Web pages may implicate the Privacy Protection Act.

This document may help in:

Assessing resources.

Developing procedures.

Assigning roles and tasks.

Considering officer safety.

Identifying and documenting equipment and supplies to bring to the scene.

Electronic Devices: Types and Potential Evidence

Chapter 1

Electronic evidence can be found in many of the new types of electronic devices available to today's consumers. This chapter displays a wide variety of the types of electronic devices commonly encountered in crime scenes, provides a general description of each type of device, and describes its common uses. In addition, it presents the potential evidence that may be found in each type of equipment.

 Many electronic devices contain memory that requires continuous power to maintain the information, such as a battery or AC power. Data can be easily lost by unplugging the power source or allowing the battery to discharge. (Note: After determining the mode of collection, collect and store the power supply adaptor or cable, if present, with the recovered device.)

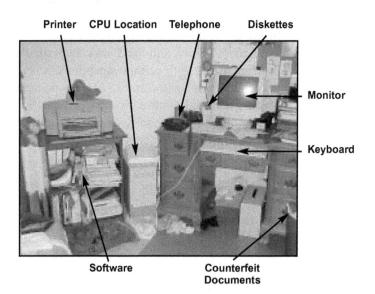

Printer   CPU Location   Telephone   Diskettes   Monitor   Keyboard   Software   Counterfeit Documents

Computer Systems

Computer

Monitor

Description: A computer system typically consists of a main base unit, sometimes called a central processing unit (CPU), data storage devices, a monitor, keyboard, and mouse. It may be a stand-alone or it may be connected to a network. There are many types of computer systems such as laptops, desktops, tower systems, modular rack-mounted systems, minicomputers, and mainframe computers. Additional components include modems, printers, scanners, docking stations, and external data storage devices. For example, a desktop is a computer system consisting of a case, motherboard, CPU, and data storage, with an external keyboard and mouse.

Laptop

Primary Uses: For all types of computing functions and information storage, including word processing, calculations, communications, and graphics.

Potential Evidence: Evidence is most commonly found in files that are stored on hard drives and storage devices and media. Examples are:

User-Created Files

User-created files may contain important evidence of criminal activity such as address books and database files that may prove criminal association, still or moving pictures that may be evidence of pedophile activity, and communications between criminals such as by e-mail or letters. Also, drug deal lists may often be found in spreadsheets.

Address books.	E-mail files.
Audio/video files.	Image/graphics files.
Calendars.	Internet bookmarks/favorites.
Database files.	Spreadsheet files.
Documents or text files.	

User-Protected Files

Port Replicator

Users have the opportunity to hide evidence in a variety of forms. For example, they may encrypt or password-protect data that are important to them. They may also hide files on a hard disk or within other files or deliberately hide incriminating evidence files under an innocuous name.

Compressed files.	Misnamed files.
Encrypted files.	Password-protected files.
Hidden files.	Steganography.

Docking Station

Evidence can also be found in files and other data areas created as a routine function of the computer's operating system. In many cases, the user is not aware that data are being written to these areas. Passwords, Internet activity, and temporary backup files are examples of data that can often be recovered and examined.

Note: There are components of files that may have evidentiary value including the date and time of creation, modification, deletion, access, user name or identification, and file attributes. Even turning the system on can modify some of this information.

Computer-Created Files

Server

Backup files.	Log files.
Configuration files.	Printer spool files.
Cookies.	Swap files.
Hidden files.	System files.
History files.	Temporary files.

Other Data Areas

Bad clusters.	Other partitions.
Computer date, time, and password.	Reserved areas.
	Slack space.
Deleted files.	Software registration information.
Free space.	
Hidden partitions.	System areas.
Lost clusters.	Unallocated space.
Metadata.	

Components

PIIIXeon Processor

Central Processing Units (CPUs)

PIII Processor

Description: Often called the "chip," it is a microprocessor located inside the computer. The microprocessor is located in the main computer box on a printed circuit board with other electronic components.

G4 Processor

Primary Uses: Performs all arithmetic and logical functions in the computer. Controls the operation of the computer.

Potential Evidence: The device itself may be evidence of component theft, counterfeiting, or remarking.

CPUs

Memory

Description: Removable circuit board(s) inside the computer. Information stored here is usually not retained when the computer is powered down.

Primary Uses: Stores user's programs and data while computer is in operation.

Memory

Potential Evidence: The device itself may be evidence of component theft, counterfeiting, or remarking.

Access Control Devices

Smart Card

Smart Cards, Dongles, Biometric Scanners

Biometric Scanner

Description: A smart card is a small handheld device that contains a microprocessor that is capable of storing a monetary value, encryption key or authentication information (password), digital certificate, or other information. A dongle is a small device that plugs into a computer port that contains types of information similar to information on a smart card. A biometric scanner is a device connected to a computer system that recognizes physical characteristics of an individual (e.g., fingerprint, voice, retina).

Parallel Dongle

USB Dongles

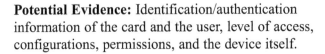

Primary Uses: Provides access control to computers or programs or functions as an encryption key.

Potential Evidence: Identification/authentication information of the card and the user, level of access, configurations, permissions, and the device itself.

Parallel Dongle

Answering Machines

Answering Machine

Description: An electronic device that is part of a telephone or connected between a telephone and the landline connection. Some models use a magnetic tape or tapes, while others use an electronic (digital) recording system.

Primary Uses: Records voice messages from callers when the called party is unavailable or chooses not to answer a telephone call. Usually plays a message from the called party before recording the message.

Note: Since batteries have a limited life, data could be lost if they fail. Therefore, appropriate personnel (e.g., evidence custodian, lab chief, forensic examiner) should be informed that a device powered by batteries is in need of immediate attention.

Potential Evidence: Answering machines can store voice messages and, in some cases, time and date information about when the message was left. They may also contain other voice recordings.

Caller identification information.	Memo.
	Phone numbers and names.
Deleted messages.	
Last number called.	Tapes.

Digital Cameras

QuickCam

Description: Camera, digital recording device for images and video, with related storage media and conversion hardware capable of transferring images and video to computer media.

11

Snappy Device (video capture device)

Primary Uses: Digital cameras capture images and/or video in a digital format that is easily transferred to computer storage media for viewing and/or editing.

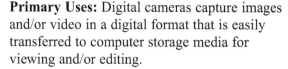

Digital Cameras

Potential Evidence:

Video Phone

Images.
Removable cartridges.
Sound.

Time and date stamp.
Video.

Handheld Devices (Personal Digital Assistants [PDAs], Electronic Organizers)

Casio PDA

Palm Cradle

Palm in Cradle

Description: A personal digital assistant (PDA) is a small device that can include computing, telephone/fax, paging, networking, and other features. It is typically used as a personal organizer. A handheld computer approaches the full functionality of a desktop computer system. Some do not contain disk drives, but may contain PC card slots that can hold a modem, hard drive, or other device. They usually include the ability to synchronize their data with other computer systems, most commonly by a connection in a cradle (see photo). If a cradle is present, attempt to locate the associated handheld device.

Primary Uses: Handheld computing, storage, and communication devices capable of storage of information.

Note: Since batteries have a limited life, data could be lost if they fail. Therefore, appropriate personnel (e.g., evidence custodian, lab chief, forensic examiner) should be informed that a device powered by batteries is in need of immediate attention.

Potential Evidence:

PDAs

Address book.
Appointment calendars/information.
Documents.
E-mail.
Handwriting.

Password.
Phone book.
Text messages.
Voice messages.

Hard Drives

Hard Drive

External Hard Drive Pack

Removable Hard Drive Tray

Description: A sealed box containing rigid platters (disks) coated with a substance capable of storing data magnetically. Can be encountered in the case of a PC as well as externally in a stand-alone case.

Primary Uses: Storage of information such as computer programs, text, pictures, video, multimedia files, etc.

Potential Evidence: See potential evidence under computer systems.

| Microdrive | 2.5-inch IDE Hard Drive w/ cover removed | 5.25-inch IDE Hard Drive (Quantum Bigfoot) | 2.5-inch IDE Hard Drive (laptop) | 3.5-inch IDE Hard Drive w/ cover removed |

Memory Cards

Memory Stick

Flash Card in PCMCIA Adaptor

Floppy Disk Adaptor/ Memory Stick

Compact Flash Card

Description: Removable electronic storage devices, which do not lose the information when power is removed from the card. It may even be possible to recover erased images from memory cards. Memory cards can store hundreds of images in a credit card-size module. Used in a variety of devices, including computers, digital cameras, and PDAs. Examples are memory sticks, smart cards, flash memory, and flash cards.

Primary Uses: Provides additional, removable methods of storing and transporting information.

Potential Evidence: See potential evidence under computer systems.

Smart Media Card

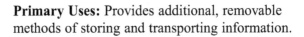
Smart Media Floppy

Memory Cards

13

Modems

External Modem

Ricochet Modem

Description: Modems, internal and external (analog, DSL, ISDN, cable), wireless modems, PC cards.

Primary Uses: A modem is used to facilitate electronic communication by allowing the computer to access other computers and/or networks via a telephone line, wireless, or other communications medium.

Potential Evidence: The device itself.

Wireless Modem

Internal Modem

PCMCIA Modem

External Modem

Network Components

Internal Network Interface Card

Local Area Network (LAN) Card or Network Interface Card (NIC)

Note: These components are indicative of a computer network. See discussion on network system evidence in chapter 5 before handling the computer system or any connected devices.

Description: Network cards, associated cables. Network cards also can be wireless.

Wireless PCMCIA Card

Primary Uses: A LAN/NIC card is used to connect computers. Cards allow for the exchange of information and resource sharing.

Wireless Network Interface Card

PCMCIA Network Interface Card

Potential Evidence: The device itself, MAC (media access control) access address.

Routers, Hubs, and Switches

Router

Ethernet Hub

Description: These electronic devices are used in networked computer systems. Routers, switches, and hubs provide a means of connecting different computers or networks. They can frequently be recognized by the presence of multiple cable connections.

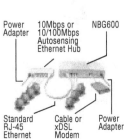

Power Adapter

10Mbps or 10/100Mbps Autosensing Ethernet Hub

NBG600

Standard RJ-45 Ethernet Cable

Cable or xDSL Modem

Power Adapter

14

Primary Uses: Equipment used to distribute and facilitate the distribution of data through networks.

Potential Evidence: The devices themselves. Also, for routers, configuration files.

CableFREE
PC Card in
a Notebook

NCF600 CableFREE
NetBlaster

NBG600

CableFREE
ISA/PCI Card
in a Desktop

Standard
RJ-45
Ethernet
Cable

Cable or
xDSL
Modem

Wireless Hub

Servers

Server

Description: A server is a computer that provides some service for other computers connected to it via a network. Any computer, including a laptop, can be configured as a server.

Primary Uses: Provides shared resources such as e-mail, file storage, Web page services, and print services for a network.

Potential Evidence: See potential evidence under computer systems.

Network Cables and Connectors

RJ-11 Phone Cable

Description: Network cables can be different colors, thicknesses, and shapes and have different connectors, depending on the components they are connected to.

Primary Uses: Connects components of a computer network.

Potential Evidence: The devices themselves.

RJ45 LAN Cable & RJ11 Phone Cable

| Centronics Printer Cable | SCSI Cable | Ultrawide SCSI Cable | Parallel Port Printer Cable | Serial Cable & Mouse |

Network Cable Dongle & PC Network Card

| PS2 Cable | PS2 Cable With PS2 AT Adapter | USB Cable With A&B Connectors | SCSI Cable | Audio/Visual Cables |

RIM Pager

Single Pager

Pagers

Pagers

Description: A handheld, portable electronic device that can contain volatile evidence (telephone numbers, voice mail, e-mail). Cell phones and personal digital assistants also can be used as paging devices.

Primary Uses: For sending and receiving electronic messages, numeric (phone numbers, etc.) and alphanumeric (text, often including e-mail).

Note: Since batteries have a limited life, data could be lost if they fail. Therefore, appropriate personnel (e.g., evidence custodian, lab chief, forensic examiner) should be informed that a device powered by batteries is in need of immediate attention.

Potential Evidence:

Address information.

E-mail.

Phone numbers.

Text messages.

Voice messages.

Multifunction Device

Inkjet Printer

Inkjet Printer

Printers

Description: One of a variety of printing systems, including thermal, laser, inkjet, and impact, connected to the computer via a cable (serial, parallel, universal serial bus (USB), firewire) or accessed via an infrared port. Some printers contain a memory buffer, allowing them to receive and store multiple page documents while they are printing. Some models may also contain a hard drive.

Primary Uses: Print text, images, etc., from the computer to paper.

Potential Evidence: Printers may maintain usage logs, time and date information, and, if attached to a network, they may store network identity information. In addition, unique characteristics may allow for identification of a printer.

Documents.

Hard drive.

Ink cartridges.

Network identity/ information.

Superimposed images on the roller.

Time and date stamp.

User usage log.

Removable Storage Devices and Media

Syquest Cartridge

External CD-ROM Drive

Recordable CD

External Zip Drive

8mm and 4mm Tapes

3.5-inch Floppy Diskette

Description: Media used to store electrical, magnetic, or digital information (e.g., floppy disks, CDs, DVDs, cartridges, tape).

Primary Uses: Portable devices that can store computer programs, text, pictures, video, multimedia files, etc.

New types of storage devices and media come on the market frequently; these are a few examples of how they appear.

Potential Evidence: See potential evidence under computer systems.

Jaz Cartridge

Zip Cartridge

DAT Tape Reader

LS-120 Floppy Disk

DLT Tape Cartridge

DVD RAM Cartridge

Tape Drive

External Media Disk Drive

Scanners

Flatbed Scanner

Sheetfed Scanner

Handheld Scanner

Description: An optical device connected to a computer, which passes a document past a scanning device (or vice versa) and sends it to the computer as a file.

Primary Uses: Converts documents, pictures, etc., to electronic files, which can then be viewed, manipulated, or transmitted on a computer.

Potential Evidence: The device itself may be evidence. Having the capability to scan may help prove illegal activity (e.g., child pornography, check fraud, counterfeiting, identity theft). In addition, imperfections such as marks on the glass may allow for unique identification of a scanner used to process documents.

Cordless

Cellular Phones

Telephones

Description: A handset either by itself (as with cell phones), or a remote base station (cordless), or connected directly to the land-line system. Draws power from an internal battery, electrical plug-in, or directly from the telephone system.

Primary Uses: Two-way communication from one instrument to another, using land lines, radio transmission, cellular systems, or a combination. Phones are capable of storing information.

Note: Since batteries have a limited life, data could be lost if they fail. Therefore, appropriate personnel (e.g., evidence custodian, lab chief, forensic examiner) should be informed that a device powered by batteries is in need of immediate attention.

Potential Evidence: Many telephones can store names, phone numbers, and caller identification information. Additionally, some cellular telephones can store appointment information, receive electronic mail and pages, and may act as a voice recorder.

Appointment calendars/information.	Password.
Caller identification information.	Phone book.
Electronic serial number.	Text messages.
E-mail.	Voice mail.
Memo.	Web browsers.

Caller ID Box

Cellular Phone Cloning Equipment

Miscellaneous Electronic Items

There are many additional types of electronic equipment that are too numerous to be listed that might be found at a crime scene. However, there are many non-traditional devices that can be an excellent source of investigative information and/or evidence. Examples are credit card skimmers, cell phone cloning equipment, caller ID boxes, audio recorders, and Web TV. Fax machines, copiers, and multifunction machines may have internal storage devices and may contain information of evidentiary value.

Cellular Phone Cloning Equipment

REMINDER: The search of this type of evidence may require a search warrant. See note in the Introduction, page 7.

Copiers

Copier

Some copiers maintain user access records and history of copies made. Copiers with the scan once/print many feature allow documents to be scanned once into memory, and then printed later.

Potential Evidence:

Documents.

Time and date stamp.

User usage log.

Credit Card Skimmers

Credit Card Skimmer

Credit card skimmers are used to read information contained on the magnetic stripe on plastic cards.

Potential Evidence: Cardholder information contained on the tracks of the magnetic stripe includes:

Card expiration date.

Credit card numbers.

User's address.

User's name.

Credit Card Skimmer

Credit Card Skimmer— Laptop

Digital Watches

There are several types of digital watches available that can function as pagers that store digital messages. They may store additional information such as address books, appointment calendars, e-mail, and notes. Some also have the capability of synchronizing information with computers.

Potential Evidence:

Address book.

Appointment calendars.

E-mail.

Notes.

Phone numbers.

Facsimile Machines

Fax Machine

Facsimile (fax) machines can store preprogrammed phone numbers and a history of transmitted and received documents. In addition, some contain memory allowing multiple-page faxes to be scanned in and sent at a later time as well as allowing incoming faxes to be held in memory and printed later. Some may store hundreds of pages of incoming and/or outgoing faxes.

Potential Evidence:

Documents.   Phone numbers.

Film cartridge.   Send/receive log.

Global Positioning Systems (GPS)

Global Positioning Systems can provide information on previous travel via destination information, way points, and routes. Some automatically store the previous destinations and include travel logs.

Potential Evidence:

Home.   Way point coordinates.

Previous destinations.   Way point name.

Travel logs.

Chapter 2

Investigative Tools and Equipment

Principle: Special tools and equipment may be required to collect electronic evidence. Experience has shown that advances in technology may dictate changes in the tools and equipment required.

Policy: There should be access to the tools and equipment necessary to document, disconnect, remove, package, and transport electronic evidence.

Procedure: Preparations should be made to acquire the equipment required to collect electronic evidence. The needed tools and equipment are dictated by each aspect of the process: documentation, collection, packaging, and transportation.

Tool Kit

Departments should have general crime scene processing tools (e.g., cameras, notepads, sketchpads, evidence forms, crime scene tape, markers). The following are additional items that may be useful at an electronic crime scene.

Documentation Tools

Cable tags.

Indelible felt tip markers.

Stick-on labels.

Disassembly and Removal Tools

A variety of nonmagnetic sizes and types of:

Flat-blade and Philips-type screwdrivers.

Hex-nut drivers.

Needle-nose pliers.

Secure-bit drivers.

Small tweezers.

Specialized screwdrivers (manufacturer-specific, e.g., Compaq, Macintosh).

Standard pliers.

Star-type nut drivers.

Wire cutters.

Package and Transport Supplies

Antistatic bags.

Antistatic bubble wrap.

Cable ties.

Evidence bags.

Evidence tape.

Packing materials (avoid materials that can produce static electricity such as styrofoam or styrofoam peanuts).

Packing tape.

Sturdy boxes of various sizes.

Other Items

Items that also should be included within a department's tool kit are:

Gloves.

Hand truck.

Large rubber bands.

List of contact telephone numbers for assistance.

Magnifying glass.

Printer paper.

Seizure disk.

Small flashlight.

Unused floppy diskettes ($3^1/_2$ and $5^1/_4$ inch).

Securing and Evaluating the Scene

Chapter 3

Principle: The first responder should take steps to ensure the safety of all persons at the scene and to protect the integrity of all evidence, both traditional and electronic.

Policy: All activities should be in compliance with departmental policy and Federal, State, and local laws. (Additional resources are referenced in appendix B.)

Procedure: After securing the scene and all persons on the scene, the first responder should visually identify potential evidence, both conventional (physical) and electronic, and determine if perishable evidence exists. The first responder should evaluate the scene and formulate a search plan.

Secure and evaluate the scene:

Follow jurisdictional policy for securing the crime scene. This would include ensuring that all persons are removed from the immediate area from which evidence is to be collected. At this point in the investigation do not alter the condition of any electronic devices: **If it is off, leave it off. If it is on, leave it on.**

Protect perishable data physically and electronically. Perishable data may be found on pagers, caller ID boxes, electronic organizers, cell phones, and other similar devices. The first responder should always keep in mind that any device containing perishable data should be immediately secured, documented, and/or photographed.

Identify telephone lines attached to devices such as modems and caller ID boxes. Document, disconnect, and label each telephone line from the wall rather than the device, when possible. There may also be other communications lines present for LAN/ethernet connections. Consult appropriate personnel/agency in these cases.

Keyboards, the computer mouse, diskettes, CDs, or other components may have latent fingerprints or other physical evidence that should be preserved. Chemicals used in processing latent prints can damage equipment and data. Therefore, latent prints should be collected after electronic evidence recovery is complete.

Conduct preliminary interviews:

Separate and identify all persons (witnesses, subjects, or others) at the scene and record their location at time of entry.

Consistent with departmental policy and applicable law, obtain from these individuals information such as:

Owners and/or users of electronic devices found at the scene, as well as passwords (see below), user names, and Internet service provider.

Passwords. Any passwords required to access the system, software, or data. (An individual may have multiple passwords, e.g., BIOS, system login, network or ISP, application files, encryption pass phrase, e-mail, access token, scheduler, or contact list.)

Purpose of the system.

Any unique security schemes or destructive devices.

Any offsite data storage.

Any documentation explaining the hardware or software installed on the system.

Chapter 4

Documenting the Scene

Principle: Documentation of the scene creates a permanent historical record of the scene. Documentation is an ongoing process throughout the investigation. It is important to accurately record the location and condition of computers, storage media, other electronic devices, and conventional evidence.

Policy: Documentation of the scene should be created and maintained in compliance with departmental policy and Federal, State, and local laws.

Procedure: The scene should be documented in detail.

Initial documentation of the physical scene:

Observe and document the physical scene, such as the position of the mouse and the location of components relative to each other (e.g., a mouse on the left side of the computer may indicate a left-handed user).

Document the condition and location of the computer system, including power status of the computer (on, off, or in sleep mode). Most computers have status lights that indicate the computer is on. Likewise, if fan noise is heard, the system is probably on. Furthermore, if the computer system is warm, that may also indicate that it is on or was recently turned off.

Identify and document related electronic components that will not be collected.

Photograph the entire scene to create a visual record as noted by the first responder. The complete room should be recorded with 360 degrees of coverage, when possible.

Photograph the **front** of the computer as well as the monitor screen and other components. Also take written notes on what appears on the monitor screen. Active programs may require videotaping or more extensive documentation of monitor screen activity.

Note: Movement of a computer system while the system is running may cause changes to system data. Therefore, the system should not be moved until it has been safely powered down as described in chapter 5.

Additional documentation of the system will be performed during the collection phase.

Evidence Collection

REMINDER: The search for and collection of evidence at an electronic crime scene may require a search warrant. See note in the Introduction, page 7.

Principle: Computer evidence, like all other evidence, must be handled carefully and in a manner that preserves its evidentiary value. This relates not just to the physical integrity of an item or device, but also to the electronic data it contains. Certain types of computer evidence, therefore, require special collection, packaging, and transportation. Consideration should be given to protect data that may be susceptible to damage or alteration from electromagnetic fields such as those generated by static electricity, magnets, radio transmitters, and other devices.

Policy: Electronic evidence should be collected according to departmental guidelines. In the absence of departmental guidelines outlining procedures for electronic evidence collection, the following procedures are suggested.

Note: Prior to collection of evidence, it is assumed that locating and documenting has been done as described in chapters 3 and 4. Recognize that other types of evidence such as trace, biological, or latent prints may exist. Follow your agency's protocol regarding evidence collection. **Destructive techniques (e.g., use of fingerprint processing chemicals) should be postponed until after electronic evidence recovery is done.**

Nonelectronic Evidence

Recovery of nonelectronic evidence can be crucial in the investigation of electronic crime. Proper care should be taken to ensure that such evidence is recovered and preserved. Items relevant to subsequent examination of electronic evidence may exist in other forms (e.g., written passwords and other handwritten notes, blank pads of paper with indented writing, hardware and software manuals, calendars, literature, text or graphical computer printouts, and photographs) and should be secured and preserved for future analysis. These items frequently are in close proximity to the computer or related hardware items. All evidence should be identified, secured, and preserved in compliance with departmental policies.

Stand-Alone and Laptop Computer Evidence

> **CAUTION:** Multiple computers may indicate a computer network. Likewise, computers located at businesses are often networked. In these situations, specialized knowledge about the system is required to effectively recover evidence and reduce your potential for civil liability. *When a computer network is encountered, contact the forensic computer expert in your department or outside consultant identified by your department for assistance.* Computer systems in a complex environment are addressed later in this chapter.

A "stand-alone" personal computer is a computer not connected to a network or other computer. Stand-alones may be desktop machines or laptops.

Laptops incorporate a computer, monitor, keyboard, and mouse into a single portable unit. Laptops differ from other computers in that they can be powered by electricity or a battery source. Therefore, they require the removal of the battery in addition to stand-alone power-down procedures.

If the computer is on, document existing conditions and call your expert or consultant. If an expert or consultant is not available, continue with the following procedure:

Procedure:

After securing the scene per chapter 3, read all steps below before taking any action (or evidentiary data may be altered).

a. Record in notes all actions you take and any changes that you observe in the monitor, computer, printer, or other peripherals that result from your actions.

b. Observe the monitor and determine if it is on, off, or in sleep mode. Then decide which of the following situations applies and follow the steps for that situation.

Situation 1: Monitor is on and work product and/or desktop is visible.

   1. Photograph screen and record information displayed.

   2. Proceed to step c.

Situation 2: Monitor is on and screen is blank (sleep mode) or screen saver (picture) is visible.

   1. Move the mouse slightly (without pushing buttons). The screen should change and show work product or request a password.

   2. If mouse movement does not cause a change in the screen, **DO NOT perform any other keystrokes or mouse operations.**

   3. Photograph the screen and record the information displayed.

   4. Proceed to step c.

Situation 3: Monitor is off.

   1. Make a note of "off" status.

   2. Turn the monitor on, then determine if the monitor status is as described in either situation 1 or 2 above and follow those steps.

c. Regardless of the power state of the computer (on, off, or sleep mode), remove the power source cable from the computer—**NOT** from the wall outlet. If dealing with a laptop, in addition to removing the power cord, remove the battery pack. The battery is removed to prevent any power to the system. Some laptops have a second battery in the multipurpose bay instead of a floppy drive or CD drive. Check for this possibility and remove that battery as well.

d. Check for outside connectivity (e.g., telephone modem, cable, ISDN, DSL). If a telephone connection is present, attempt to identify the telephone number.

e. To avoid damage to potential evidence, remove any floppy disks that are present, package the disk separately, and label the package. If available, insert either a seizure disk or a blank floppy disk. Do **NOT** remove CDs or touch the CD drive.

f. Place tape over all the drive slots and over the power connector.

g. Record make, model, and serial numbers.

h. Photograph and diagram the connections of the computer and the corresponding cables.

i. Label all connectors and cable ends (including connections to peripheral devices) to allow for exact reassembly at a later time. Label unused connection ports as "unused." Identify laptop computer docking stations in an effort to identify other storage media.

j. Record or log evidence according to departmental procedures.

k. If transport is required, package the components as fragile cargo (see chapter 6).

Computers in a Complex Environment

Business environments frequently have multiple computers connected to each other, to a central server, or both. Securing and processing a crime scene where the computer systems are networked poses special problems, as improper shutdown may destroy data. This can result in loss of evidence and potential severe civil liability. When investigating criminal activity in a known business environment, the presence of a computer network should be planned for in advance, if possible, and appropriate expert assistance obtained. It should be noted that computer networks can also be found in a home environment and the same concerns exist.

10Base2 Connector

The possibility of various operating systems and complex hardware configurations requiring different shutdown procedures make the processing of a network crime scene beyond the scope of this guide. However, it is important that computer networks be recognized and identified, so that expert assistance can be obtained if one is encountered. Appendix C provides a list of technical resources that can be contacted for assistance.

10BaseT Connector

Indications that a computer network may be present include:

The presence of multiple computer systems.

The presence of cables and connectors, such as those depicted in the pictures at left, running between computers or central devices such as hubs.

Information provided by informants or individuals at the scene.

The presence of network components as depicted in chapter 1.

Other Electronic Devices and Peripheral Evidence

The electronic devices such as the ones in the list below may contain potential evidence associated with criminal activity. Unless an emergency exists, the device should not be operated. Should it be necessary to access information from the device, all actions associated with the manipulation of the device should be documented to preserve the authenticity of the information. Many of the items listed below may contain data that could be lost if not handled properly. For more detailed information on these devices, see chapter 1.

Examples of other electronic devices (including computer peripherals):

Audio recorders.

Answering machines.

Cables.

Caller ID devices.

Cellular telephones.

Chips. (When components such as chips are found in quantity, it may be indicative of chip theft.)

Copy machines.

Databank/Organizer digital.

Digital cameras (still and video).

Dongle or other hardware protection devices (keys) for software.

Drive duplicators.

External drives.

Fax machines.

Flash memory cards.

Floppies, diskettes, CD–ROMs.

GPS devices.

Pagers.

Palm Pilots/electronic organizers.

PCMCIA cards.

Printers (if active, allow to complete printing).

Removable media.

Scanners (film, flatbed, watches, etc.).

Smart cards/secure ID tokens.

Telephones (including speed dialers, etc.).

VCRs.

Wireless access point.

Note: When seizing removable media, ensure that you take the associated device that created the media (e.g., tape drive, cartridge drives such as Zip®, Jaz®, ORB, Clik!™, Syquest, LS-120).

Packaging, Transportation, and Storage

Chapter 6

Principle: Actions taken should not add, modify, or destroy data stored on a computer or other media. Computers are fragile electronic instruments that are sensitive to temperature, humidity, physical shock, static electricity, and magnetic sources. Therefore, special precautions should be taken when packaging, transporting, and storing electronic evidence. To maintain chain of custody of electronic evidence, document its packaging, transportation, and storage.

Policy: Ensure that proper procedures are followed for packaging, transporting, and storing electronic evidence to avoid alteration, loss, physical damage, or destruction of data.

Packaging procedure:

a. Ensure that all collected electronic evidence is properly documented, labeled, and inventoried before packaging.

b. Pay special attention to latent or trace evidence and take actions to preserve it.

c. Pack magnetic media in antistatic packaging (paper or antistatic plastic bags). Avoid using materials that can produce static electricity, such as standard plastic bags.

d. Avoid folding, bending, or scratching computer media such as diskettes, CD–ROMs, and tapes.

e. Ensure that all containers used to hold evidence are properly labeled.

Note: If multiple computer systems are collected, label each system so that it can be reassembled as found (e.g., System A–mouse, keyboard, monitor, main base unit; System B–mouse, keyboard, monitor, main base unit).

Transportation procedure:

a. Keep electronic evidence away from magnetic sources. Radio transmitters, speaker magnets, and heated seats are examples of items that can damage electronic evidence.

b. Avoid storing electronic evidence in vehicles for prolonged periods of time. Conditions of excessive heat, cold, or humidity can damage electronic evidence.

c. Ensure that computers and other components that are not packaged in containers are secured in the vehicle to avoid shock and excessive vibrations. For example, computers may be placed on the vehicle floor and monitors placed on the seat with the screen down and secured by a seat belt.

d. Maintain the chain of custody on all evidence transported.

Storage procedure:

a. Ensure that evidence is inventoried in accordance with departmental policies.

b. Store evidence in a secure area away from temperature and humidity extremes. Protect it from magnetic sources, moisture, dust, and other harmful particles or contaminants.

Note: Be aware that potential evidence such as dates, times, and systems configurations may be lost as a result of prolonged storage. Since batteries have a limited life, data could be lost if they fail. Therefore, appropriate personnel (e.g., evidence custodian, lab chief, forensic examiner) should be informed that a device powered by batteries is in need of immediate attention.

Chapter 7

Forensic Examination by Crime Category

The following outline should help officers/investigators identify the common findings of a forensic examination as they relate to specific crime categories. This outline will also help define the scope of the examination to be performed. (This information is also presented as a matrix at the end of this chapter.)

Auction Fraud (Online)

Account data regarding online auction sites.

Accounting/bookkeeping software and associated data files.

Address books.

Calendar.

Chat logs.

Customer information/credit card data.

Databases.

Digital camera software.

E-mail/notes/letters.

Financial/asset records.

Image files.

Internet activity logs.

Internet browser history/cache files.

Online financial institution access software.

Records/documents of "testimonials."

Telephone records.

Child Exploitation/Abuse

Chat logs.

Date and time stamps.

Digital camera software.

E-mail/notes/letters.

Games.

Graphic editing and viewing software.

Images.

Internet activity logs.

Movie files.

User-created directory and file names that classify images.

Computer Intrusion

Address books.

Configuration files.

E-mail/notes/letters.

Executable programs.

Internet activity logs.

Internet protocol (IP) address and user name.

Internet relay chat (IRC) logs.

Source code.

Text files (user names and passwords).

Death Investigation

Address books.

Diaries.

E-mail/notes/letters.

Financial/asset records.

Images.

Internet activity logs.

Legal documents and wills.

Medical records.

Telephone records.

Domestic Violence

Address books.

Diaries.

E-mail/notes/letters.

Financial/asset records.

Medical records.

Telephone records.

Economic Fraud (Including Online Fraud, Counterfeiting)

Address books.

Calendar.

Check, currency, and money order images.

Credit card skimmers.

Customer information/credit card data.

Databases.

E-mail/notes/letters.

False financial transaction forms.

False identification.

Financial/asset records.

Images of signatures.

Internet activity logs.

Online financial institution access software.

35

E-Mail Threats/Harassment/Stalking

Address books.

Diaries.

E-mail/notes/letters.

Financial/asset records.

Images.

Internet activity logs.

Legal documents.

Telephone records.

Victim background research.

Extortion

Date and time stamps.

E-mail/notes/letters.

History log.

Internet activity logs.

Temporary Internet files.

User names.

Gambling

Address books.

Calendar.

Customer database and player records.

Customer information/credit card data.

Electronic money.

E-mail/notes/letters.

Financial/asset records.

Image players.

Internet activity logs.

Online financial institution access software.

Sports betting statistics.

Identity Theft

Hardware and software tools.

Backdrops.

Credit card generators.

Credit card reader/writer.

Digital cameras.

Scanners.

Identification templates.

Birth certificates.

Check cashing cards.

Digital photo images for photo identification.

Driver's license.

Electronic signatures.

Fictitious vehicle registrations.

Proof of auto insurance documents.

Scanned signatures.

Social security cards.

Internet activity related to ID theft.

E-mails and newsgroup postings.

Erased documents.

Online orders.

Online trading information.

System files and file slack.

World Wide Web activity at forgery sites.

Negotiable instruments.

Business checks.

Cashiers checks.

Counterfeit money.

Credit card numbers.

Fictitious court documents.

Fictitious gift certificates.

Fictitious loan documents.

Fictitious sales receipts.

Money orders.

Personal checks.

Stock transfer documents.

Travelers checks.

Vehicle transfer documentation.

Narcotics

Address books.

Calendar.

Databases.

Drug recipes.

E-mail/notes/letters.

False identification.

Financial/asset records.

Internet activity logs.

Prescription form images.

Prostitution

Address books.

Biographies.

Calendar.

Customer database/records.

E-mail/notes/letters.

False identification.

Financial/asset records.

Internet activity logs.

Medical records.

World Wide Web page advertising.

Software Piracy

Chat logs.

E-mail/notes/letters.

Image files of software certificates.

Internet activity logs.

Serial numbers.

Software cracking information and utilities.

User-created directory and file names that classify copyrighted software.

At a physical scene, look for duplication and packaging material.

Telecommunications Fraud

Cloning software.

Customer database/records.

Electronic Serial Number (ESN)/Mobile Identification Number (MIN) pair records.

E-mail/notes/letters.

Financial/asset records.

"How to phreak" manuals.

Internet activity.

Telephone records.

The following information, when available, should be documented to assist in the forensic examination:

Case summary.

Internet protocol address(es).

Keyword lists.

Nicknames.

Passwords.

Points of contact.

Supporting documents.

Type of crime.

	Sex Crimes		Crimes Against Persons			Fraud/Other Financial Crime								
	Child Exploitation/Abuse	Prostitution	Death Investigation	Domestic Violence	E-Mail Threats/Harassment/Stalking	Auction Fraud	Computer Intrusion	Economic Fraud	Extortion	Gambling	Identity Theft	Narcotics	Software Piracy	Telecommunications Fraud
General Information:														
Databases														
E-Mail/notes/letters														
Financial/asset records														
Medical records														
Telephone records														
Specific Information:														
Account data														
Accounting/bookkeeping software														
Address books														
Backdrops														
Biographies														
Birth certificates														
Calendar														
Chat logs														
Check, currency, and money order images														
Check cashing cards														
Cloning software														
Configuration files														
Counterfeit money														
Credit card generators														
Credit card numbers														
Credit card reader/writer														
Credit card skimmers														
Customer database/records														
Customer information/credit card data														
Date and time stamps														
Diaries														
Digital cameras/software/images														
Driver's license														
Drug recipes														
Electronic money														
Electronic signatures														

Specific Information (Cont):

	Sex Crimes		Crimes Against Persons			Fraud/Other Financial Crime								
	Child Exploitation/Abuse	Prostitution	Death Investigation	Domestic Violence	E-Mail Threats/Harassment/Stalking	Auction Fraud	Computer Intrusion	Economic Fraud	Extortion	Gambling	Identity Theft	Narcotics	Software Piracy	Telecommunications Fraud
Erased Internet documents														
ESN/MIN pair records														
Executable programs														
False financial transaction forms														
False identification														
Fictitious court documents														
Fictitious gift certificates														
Fictitious loan documents														
Fictitious sales receipts														
Fictitious vehicle registrations														
Games														
Graphic editing and viewing software														
History log														
"How to phreak" manuals														
Images														
Images of signatures														
Image files of software certificates														
Image players														
Internet activity logs														
Internet browser history/cache files														
IP address and user name														
IRC chat logs														
Legal documents and wills														
Movie files														
Online financial institution access software														
Online orders and trading information														
Prescription form images														
Records/documents of "testimonials"														

(Continued)

	Sex Crimes		Crimes Against Persons			Fraud/Other Financial Crime								
	Child Exploitation/Abuse	Prostitution	Death Investigation	Domestic Violence	E-Mail Threats/Harassment/Stalking	Auction Fraud	Computer Intrusion	Economic Fraud	Extortion	Gambling	Identity Theft	Narcotics	Software Piracy	Telecommunications Fraud
Specific Information (Cont):														
Scanners/scanned signatures														
Serial numbers														
Social security cards														
Software cracking information and utilities														
Source code														
Sports betting statistics														
Stock transfer documents														
System files and file slack														
Temporary Internet files														
User names														
User-created directory and file names that classify copyrighted software														
User-created directory and file names that classify images														
Vehicle insurance and transfer documentation														
Victim background research														
Web activity at forgery sites														
Web page advertising														

The views and opinions of authors expressed herein do not necessarily reflect those of the United States Government.

Reference herein to any specific commercial products, processes, or services by trade name, trademark, manufacturer, or otherwise does not necessarily constitute or imply its endorsement, recommendation, or favoring by the United States Government.

The information and statements contained in this document shall not be used for the purposes of advertising or to imply the endorsement or recommendation of the United States Government.

With respect to information contained in this publication, neither the United States Government nor any of its employees make any warranty, express or implied, including but not limited to the warranties of merchantability and fitness for a particular purpose. Further, neither the United States Government nor any of its employees assume any legal liability or responsibility for the accuracy, completeness, or usefulness of any information, apparatus, product, or process disclosed; nor do they represent that its use would not infringe on privately owned rights.

Glossary

Access token: In Windows NT, an internal security card that is generated when users log on. It contains the security IDs (SIDs) for the user and all the groups to which the user belongs. A copy of the access token is assigned to every process launched by the user.

BIOS: Basic Input Output System. The set of routines stored in read-only memory that enable a computer to start the operating system and to communicate with the various devices in the system such as disk drives, keyboard, monitor, printer, and communication ports.

Buffer: An area of memory, often referred to as a "cache," used to speed up access to devices. It is used for temporary storage of data read from or waiting to be sent to a device such as a hard disk, CD-ROM, printer, or tape drive.

Clik!™: A portable disk drive, also known as a PocketZip disk. The external drive connects to the computer via the USB port or a PC card, the latter containing a removable cartridge slot within the card itself.

CD-R: Compact disk-recordable. A disk to which data can be written but not erased.

CD-RW: Compact disk-rewritable. A disk to which data can be written and erased.

Compressed file: A file that has been reduced in size through a compression algorithm to save disk space. The act of compressing a file will make it unreadable to most programs until the file is uncompressed.

Cookies: Small text files stored on a computer while the user is browsing the Internet. These little pieces of data store information such as e-mail identification, passwords, and history of pages the user has visited.

CPU: Central processing unit. The computational and control unit of a computer. Located inside a computer, it is the "brain" that performs all arithmetic, logic, and control functions in a computer.

Deleted files: If a subject knows there are incriminating files on the computer, he or she may delete them in an effort to eliminate the evidence. Many computer users think that this actually eliminates the information. However, depending on how the files are deleted, in many instances a forensic examiner is able to recover all or part of the original data.

Digital evidence: Information stored or transmitted in binary form that may be relied upon in court.

Docking station: A device to which a laptop or notebook computer can be attached for use as a desktop computer, usually having a connector for externally connected devices such as hard drives, scanners, keyboards, monitors, and printers.

Documentation: Written notes, audio/videotapes, printed forms, sketches, and/or photographs that form a detailed record of the scene, evidence recovered, and actions taken during the search of the scene.

Dongle: Also called a hardware key, a dongle is a copy protection device supplied with software that plugs into a computer port, often the parallel port on a PC. The software sends a code to that port and the key responds by reading out its serial number, which verifies its presence to the program. The key hinders software duplication because each copy of the program is tied to a unique number, which is difficult to obtain, and the key has to be programmed with that number.

DSL: Digital subscriber line. Protocols designed to allow high-speed data communication over the existing telephone lines between end-users and telephone companies.

Duplicate digital evidence: A duplicate is an accurate digital reproduction of all data objects contained on the original physical item.

DVD: Digital versatile disk. Similar in appearance to a compact disk, but can store larger amounts of data.

Electromagnetic fields: The field of force associated with electric charge in motion having both electric and magnetic components and containing a definite amount of electromagnetic energy. Examples of devices that produce electromagnetic fields include speakers and radio transmitters frequently found in the trunk of the patrol car.

Electronic device: A device that operates on principles governing the behavior of electrons. See chapter 1 for examples, which include computer systems, scanners, printers, etc.

Electronic evidence: Electronic evidence is information and data of investigative value that is stored on or transmitted by an electronic device.

Encryption: Any procedure used in cryptography to convert plain text into ciphertext in order to prevent anyone but the intended recipient from reading that data.

First responder: The initial responding law enforcement officer and/or other public safety official arriving at the scene.

Hidden data: Many computer systems include an option to protect information from the casual user by hiding it. A cursory examination may not display hidden files, directories, or partitions to the untrained viewer. A forensic examination will document the presence of this type of information.

ISDN: Integrated services digital network. A high-speed digital telephone line for high-speed network communications.

ISP: Internet service provider. An organization that provides access to the Internet. Small Internet service providers provide service via modem and ISDN, while the larger ones also offer private line hookups (e.g., T1, fractional T1).

Jaz®: A high-capacity removable hard disk system.

Latent: Present, although not visible, but capable of becoming visible.

LS-120: Laser Servo-120 is a floppy disk technology that holds 120MB. LS-120 drives use a dual-gap head, which reads and writes 120MB disks as well as standard 3.5-inch 1.44MB and 720KB floppies.

Magnetic media: A disk, tape, cartridge, diskette, or cassette that is used to store data magnetically.

Misnamed files and files with altered extensions: One simple way to disguise a file's contents is to change the file's name to something innocuous. For example, if an investigator was looking for spreadsheets by searching for a particular file extension, such as ".XLS," a file whose extension had been changed by the user to ".DOC" would not appear as a result of the search. Forensic examiners use special techniques to determine if this has occurred, which the casual user would not normally be aware of.

Modem: A device used by computers to communicate over telephone lines. It is recognized by connection to a phone line.

Network: A group of computers connected to one another to share information and resources.

Networked system: A computer connected to a network.

ORB: A high-capacity removable hard disk system. ORB drives use magnetoresistive (MR) read/write head technology.

Original electronic evidence: Physical items and those data objects that are associated with those items at the time of seizure.

Password-protected files: Many software programs include the ability to protect a file using a password. One type of password protection is sometimes called "access denial." If this feature is used, the data will be present on the disk in the normal manner, but the software program will not open or display the file without the user entering the password. In many cases, forensic examiners are able to bypass this feature.

Peripheral devices: An auxiliary device such as a printer, modem, or data storage system that works in conjunction with a computer.

Phreaking: Telephone hacking.

Port: An interface by which a computer communicates with another device or system. Personal computers have various types of ports. Internally, there are several ports for connecting disk drives, display screens, and keyboards. Externally, personal computers have ports for connecting modems, printers, mice, and other peripheral devices.

Port replicator: A device containing common PC ports such as serial, parallel, and network ports that plugs into a notebook computer. A port replicator is similar to a docking station but docking stations normally provide capability for additional expansion boards.

Printer spool files: Print jobs that are not printed directly are stored in spool files on disk.

Removable media: Items (e.g., floppy disks, CDs, DVDs, cartridges, tape) that store data and can be easily removed.

Screen saver: A utility program that prevents a monitor from being etched by an unchanging image. It also can provide access control.

Seizure disk: A specially prepared floppy disk designed to protect the computer system from accidental alteration of data.

Server: A computer that provides some service for other computers connected to it via a network.

Sleep mode: Power conservation status that suspends the hard drive and monitor resulting in a blank screen to conserve energy, sometimes referred to as suspend mode.

Stand-alone computer: A computer not connected to a network or other computer.

Steganography: The art and science of communicating in a way that hides the existence of the communication. It is used to hide a file inside another. For example, a child pornography image can be hidden inside another graphic image file, audio file, or other file format.

System administrator: The individual who has legitimate supervisory rights over a computer system. The administrator maintains the highest access to the system. Also can be known as sysop, sysadmin, and system operator.

Temporary and swap files: Many computers use operating systems and applications that store data temporarily on the hard drive. These files, which are generally hidden and inaccessible, may contain information that the investigator finds useful.

USB: Universal Serial Bus. A hardware interface for low-speed peripherals such as the keyboard, mouse, joystick, scanner, printer, and telephony devices.

Volatile memory: Memory that loses its content when power is turned off or lost.

Zip®: A 3.5-inch removable disk drive. The drive is bundled with software that can catalog disks and lock the files for security.

Legal Resources List

Publications

Searching and Seizing Computers and Obtaining Electronic Evidence in Criminal Investigations. Washington, D.C.: U.S. Department of Justice, Computer Crime and Intellectual Property Section, March 2001. (Online under http://www.cybercrime.gov/searchmanual.htm.)

Prosecuting Cases That Involve Computers: A Resource for State and Local Prosecutors (CD-ROM), National White Collar Crime Center, 2001. (See http://www.nctp.org and http://www.training.nw3c.org for information).

Web Sites

Computer Crime and Intellectual Property Section of the U.S. Department of Justice, 202–514–1026, http://www.cybercrime.gov.

National Cybercrime Training Partnership, 877–628–7674, http://www.nctp.org.

Infobin, http://www.infobin.org/cfid/isplist.htm.

Technical Resources List

National

**Computer Analysis
  Response Team**
FBI Laboratory
935 Pennsylvania Avenue N.W.
Washington, DC 20535
Phone: 202–324–9307
http://www.fbi.gov/programs/lab/
  org/cart.htm

High Tech Crime Consortium
International Headquarters
1506 North Stevens Street
Tacoma, WA 98406–3826
Phone: 253–752–2427
Fax: 253–752–2430
E-mail:
admin@hightechcrimecops.org
http://www.HighTechCrimeCops.org

**Information Systems Security
  Association (ISSA)**
7044 South 13th Street
Oak Creek, WI 53154
Phone: 800–370–4772
http://www.issa.org

Internal Revenue Service
Criminal Investigation Division
Rich Mendrop
Computer Investigative Specialist
Program Manager
2433 South Kirkwood Court
Denver, CO 80222
Phone: 303–756–0646
E-mail: richard.mendrop@ci.irs.gov

**National Aeronautics and Space
  Administration**
Cheri Carr
Computer Forensic Lab Chief
NASA Office of the Inspector
  General
Network and Advanced
  Technology Protections Office
300 E Street S.W.
Washington, DC 20546
Phone: 202–358–4298

**National Aeronautics and Space
  Administration**
Charles Coe
Director of Technical Services
NASA Office of the Inspector
  General
Network and Advanced
  Technology Protections Office
300 E Street S.W.
Washington, DC 20546
Phone: 202–358–2573

**National Aeronautics and Space
  Administration**
Steve Nesbitt
Director of Operations
NASA Office of the Inspector
  General
Network and Advanced
  Technology Protections Office
300 E Street S.W.
Washington, DC 20546
Phone: 202–358–2576

National Center for Forensic Science
University of Central Florida
P.O. Box 162367
Orlando, FL 32816
Phone: 407–823–6469
Fax: 407–823–3162
http://www.ncfs.ucf.edu

National Criminal Justice Computer Laboratory and Training Center SEARCH Group, Inc.
7311 Greenhaven Drive, Suite 145
Sacramento, CA 95831
Phone: 916–392–2550
http://www.search.org

National Law Enforcement and Corrections Technology Center (NLECTC)–Northeast
26 Electronic Parkway
Rome, NY 13441
Phone: 888–338–0584
Fax: 315–330–4315
http://www.nlectc.org

National Law Enforcement and Corrections Technology Center (NLECTC)–West
c/o The Aerospace Corporation
2350 East El Segundo Boulevard
El Segundo, CA 90245
Phone: 888–548–1618
Fax: 310–336–2227
http://www.nlectc.org

National Railroad Passenger Corporation (NRPC) (AMTRAK)
Office of Inspector General
Office of Investigations
William D. Purdy
Senior Special Agent
10 G Street N.E., Suite 3E–400
Washington, DC 20002
Phone: 202–906–4318
E-mail: oigagent@aol.com

National White Collar Crime Center
7401 Beaufont Springs Drive
Richmond, VA 23225
Phone: 800–221–4424
http://www.nw3c.org

Scientific Working Group on Digital Evidence
http://www.for-swg.org/swgdein.htm

Social Security Administration
Office of Inspector General
Electronic Crime Team
4–S–1 Operations Building
6401 Security Boulevard
Baltimore, MD 21235
Phone: 410–965–7421
Fax: 410–965–5705

U.S. Customs Service's Cyber Smuggling Center
11320 Random Hills, Suite 400
Fairfax, VA 22030
Phone: 703–293–8005
Fax: 703–293–9127

U.S. Department of Defense
DoD Computer Forensics Laboratory
911 Elkridge Landing Road, Suite 300
Linthicum, MD 21090
Phone: 410–981–0100/877–981–3235

U.S. Department of Defense
Office of Inspector General
Defense Criminal Investigative Service
David E. Trosch
Special Agent
Program Manager, Computer Forensics Program
400 Army Navy Drive
Arlington, VA 22202
Phone: 703–604–8733
E-mail: dtrosch@dodig.osd.mil
http://www.dodig.osd.mil/dcis/dcismain.html

U.S. Department of Energy
Office of the Inspector General
Technology Crimes Section
1000 Independence Avenue, 5A–235
Washington, DC 20585
Phone: 202–586–9939
Fax: 202–586–0754
E-mail: tech.crime@hq.doe.gov

U.S. Department of Justice
Criminal Division
Computer Crime and Intellectual
   Property Section (CCIPS)
Duty Attorney
1301 New York Avenue N.W.
Washington, DC 20530
Phone: 202–514–1026
http://www.cybercrime.gov

U.S. Department of Justice
Drug Enforcement Administration
Michael J. Phelan
Group Supervisor
Computer Forensics
Special Testing and Research Lab
10555 Furnace Road
Lorton, VA 22079
Phone: 703–495–6787
Fax: 703–495–6794
E-mail: mphelan@erols.com

U.S. Department of Transportation
Office of Inspector General
Jacquie Wente
Special Agent
111 North Canal, Suite 677
Chicago, IL 60606
Phone: 312–353–0106
E-mail: wentej@oig.dot.gov

U.S. Department of the Treasury
Bureau of Alcohol, Tobacco and Firearms
Technical Support Division
Visual Information Branch
Jack L. Hunter, Jr.
Audio and Video Forensic Enhancement
   Specialist
650 Massachusetts Avenue N.W.
Room 3220
Washington, DC 20226–0013
Phone: 202–927–8037
Fax: 202–927–8682
E-mail: jlhunter@atfhq.atf.treas.gov

U. S. Postal Inspection Service
Digital Evidence
22433 Randolph Drive
Dulles, VA 20104–1000
Phone: 703–406–7927

U.S. Secret Service
Electronic Crimes Branch
950 H Street N.W.
Washington, DC 20223
Phone: 202–406–5850
Fax: 202–406–9233

Veterans Affairs
Office of the Inspector General
Robert Friel
Program Director, Computer Crimes
   and Forensics
801 I Street N.W., Suite 1064
Washington, DC 20001
Phone: 202–565–5701
E-mail: robert.friel@mail.va.gov

By State

Alabama

Alabama Attorney General's Office
Donna White, S/A
11 South Union Street
Montgomery, AL 36130
Phone: 334–242–7345
E-mail: dwhite@ago.state.al.us

Alabama Bureau of Investigation
Internet Crimes Against Children Unit
Glenn Taylor
Agent
716 Arcadia Circle
Huntsville, AL 35801
Phone: 256–539–4028
E-mail: tgtjr@aol.com

Homewood Police Department
Wade Morgan
1833 29th Avenue South
Homewood, AL 35209
Phone: 205–877–8637
E-mail: morgan64@bellsouth.net

Hoover Police Department
Det. Michael Alexiou
FBI Innocent Images Task Force,
  Birmingham
100 Municipal Drive
Hoover, AL 35216
Phone: 205–444–7798
Pager: 205–819–0507
Mobile: 205–567–7516
E-mail: alexioum@ci.hoover.al.us

Alaska

Alaska State Troopers
Sgt. Curt Harris
White Collar Crime Section
5700 East Tudor Road
Anchorage, AK 99507
Phone: 907–269–5627
E-mail: curtis_harris@dps.state.ak.us

Anchorage Police Department
Det. Glen Klinkhart/Sgt. Ross Plummer
4501 South Bragaw Street
Anchorage, AK 99507–1599
Phone: 907–786–8767/907–786–8778
E-mail: gklinkhart@ci.anchorage.ak.us
  rplummer@ci.us.ak.gov

University of Alaska at Fairbanks
  Police Department
Marc Poeschel
Coordinator
P.O. Box 755560
Fairbanks, AK 99775
Phone: 907–474–7721
E-mail: fyglock@uaf.edu

Arizona

Arizona Attorney General's Office
Technology Crimes
1275 West Washington Street
Phoenix, AZ 85007
Phone: 602–542–3881
Fax: 602–542–5997

Arkansas

University of Arkansas at Little Rock Police Department
William (Bill) Reardon/Bobby Floyd
2801 South University Avenue
Little Rock, AR 72204
Phone: 501–569–8793/501–569–8794
E-mail: wcreardon@ualr.edu
     bcfloyd@ualr.edu

California

Bureau of Medi-Cal Fraud and Elder Abuse
Luis Salazar
Senior Legal Analyst/Computer Forensic
  Team Coordinator
110 West A Street, Suite 1100
San Diego, CA 92101
Phone: 619–645–2432
Fax: 619–645–2455
E-mail: SALAZAL@hdcdojnet.state.ca.us

California Franchise Tax Board
Investigations Bureau
Ashraf L. Massoud
Special Agent
100 North Barranca Street, Suite 600
West Covina, CA 91791–1600
Phone: 626–859–4678
E-mail: ashraf_massoud@ftb.ca.gov

Kern County Sheriff's Department
Tom Fugitt
1350 Norris Road
Bakersfield, CA 93308
Phone: 661–391–7728
E-mail: fugitt@co.kern.ca.us

Los Angeles Police Department
Computer Crime Unit
Det. Terry D. Willis
150 North Los Angeles Street
Los Angeles, CA 90012
Phone: 213–485–3795

Modesto Police Department
600 10th Street
Modesto, CA 95353
Phone: 209–572–9500, ext. 29119

North Bay High Technology Evidence Analysis Team (HEAT)
Sgt. Dave Bettin
1125 Third Street
Napa, CA 94559
Phone: 707–253–4500

Regional Computer Forensic Laboratory at San Diego
9797 Aero Drive
San Diego, CA 92123–1800
Phone: 858–499–7799
Fax: 858–499–7798
E-mail: rcfl@rcfl.org
http://www.rcfl.org

Sacramento Valley Hi-Tech Crimes Task Force
Hi-Tech Crimes Division
Sacramento County Sheriff's Department
Lt. Mike Tsuchida
P.O. Box 988
Sacramento, CA 95812–0998
Phone: 916–874–3030
E-mail: miket@sna.com

San Diego High Technology Crimes Economic Fraud Division
David Decker
District Attorney's Office, County of
  San Diego
Suite 1020
San Diego, CA 92101
Phone: 619–531–3660
E-mail: ddecke@sdcda.org

Silicon Valley High Tech Crime Task Force
Rapid Enforcement Allied Computer Team (REACT)
c/o Federal Bureau of Investigation
Nick Muyo
950 South Bascom Avenue, Suite 3011
San Jose, CA 95128
Phone: 408–494–7161
Pager: 408–994–3264
E-mail: sharx91@aol.com

Southern California High Technology Crime Task Force
Sgt. Woody Gish
Commercial Crimes Bureau
Los Angeles County Sheriff's Department
11515 South Colima Road, Room M104
Whittier, CA 90604
Phone: 562–946–7942

U.S. Customs Service
Frank Day
Senior Special Agent
Computer Investigative Specialist
3403 10th Street, Suite 600
Riverside, CA 92501
Phone: 906–276–6664, ext. 231
E-mail: FDay@usa.net

Colorado

Denver District Attorney's Office
Henry R. Reeve
General Counsel/Deputy D.A.
303 West Colfax Avenue, Suite 1300
Denver, CO 80204
Phone: 720–913–9000

Department of Public Safety
Colorado Bureau of Investigation
Computer Crime Investigation
690 Kipling Street, Suite 3000
Denver, Colorado 80215
Phone: 303–239–4292
Fax: 303–239–5788
E-mail: Collin.Reese@cdps.state.co.us

Connecticut

Connecticut Department of Public Safety
Division of Scientific Services
Forensic Science Laboratory
Computer Crimes and Electronic Evidence Unit
278 Colony Street
Meriden, CT 06451
Phone: 203–639–6492
Fax: 203–630–3760
E-mail: arussell@nwc3.org

Connecticut Department of Revenue Services
Special Investigations Section
25 Sigourney Street
Hartford, CT 06106
Phone: 860–297–5877
Fax: 860–297–5625
E-mail: Cal.Mellor@po.state.ct.us

Yale University Police Department
Sgt. Dan Rainville
98–100 Sachem Street
New Haven, CT 06511
Phone: 203–432–7958
E-mail: daniel.rainville@yale.edu

Delaware

Delaware State Police
High Technology Crimes Unit
1575 McKee Road, Suite 204
Dover, DE 19904
Det. Steve Whalen
Phone: 302–739–2761
E-mail: swhalen@state.de.us
Det. Daniel Willey
Phone: 302–739–8020
E-mail: dawilley@state.de.us
Sgt. Robert Moses
Phone: 302–739–2467
E-Mail: romoses@state.de.us
Capt. David Citro
Phone: 302–734–1399
E-mail: dcitro@state.de.us

New Castle County Police Department
Criminal Investigations Unit
Det. Christopher M. Shanahan/
   Det. Edward E. Whatley
3601 North DuPont Highway
New Castle, DE 19720
Phone: 302–395–8110
E-mail: cshanahan@co.new-castle.de.us
           eewhatley@co.new-castle.de.us

University of Delaware Police
Department
Capt. Stephen M. Bunting
101 MOB
700 Pilottown Road
Lewes, DE 19958
Phone: 302–645–4334
E-mail: sbunting@udel.edu

District of Columbia

Metropolitan Police Department
Special Investigations Division
Computer Crimes and Forensics Unit
Investigator Tim Milloff
300 Indiana Avenue N.W., Room 3019
Washington, DC 20001
Phone: 202–727–4252/202–727–1010
E-mail: tmiloff@leo.gov

Florida

Florida Atlantic University Police
Department
Det. Wilfredo Hernandez
777 Glades Road, #49
Boca Raton, FL 33431
Phone: 561–297–2371
Fax: 561–297–3565

Gainsville Police Department
Criminal Investigations/Computer Unit
Det. Jim Ehrat
721 N.W. Sixth Street
Gainsville, FL 32601
Phone: 352–334–2488
E-mail: ehratjj@ci.gainesville.fl.us

Institute of Police Technology and
Management
Computer Forensics Laboratory
University of North Florida
12000 Alumni Drive
Jacksonville, FL 32224–2678
Phone: 904–620–4786
Fax: 904–620–2453
http://www.iptm.org

Office of Statewide Prosecution
High Technology Crimes
Thomas A. Sadaka
Special Counsel
135 West Central Boulevard, Suite 1000
Orlando, FL 32801
Phone: 407–245–0893
Fax: 407–245–0356

Pinellas County Sheriff's Office
Det. Matthew Miller
10750 Ulmerton Road
Largo, FL 33778
E-mail: mxmiller@co.pinellas.fl.us

Georgia

Georgia Bureau of Investigation
Financial Investigations Unit
Steve Edwards
Special Agent in Charge
5255 Snapfinger Drive, Suite 150
Decatur, GA 30035
Phone: 770–987–2323
Fax: 770–987–9775
E-mail: steve.edwards@GBI.state.ga.us

Hawaii

Honolulu Police Department
White Collar Crime Unit
Det. Chris Duque
801 South Beretania Street
Honolulu, HI 96819
Phone: 808–529–3112

Idaho

Ada County Sheriff's Office
Det. Lon Anderson, CFCE
7200 Barrister Drive
Boise, ID 83704
Phone: 208–377–6691

Illinois

Illinois State Police
Computer Crimes Investigation Unit
Division of Operations
Operational Services Command
Statewide Special Investigations Bureau
500 Illes Park Place, Suite 104
Springfield, IL 62718
Phone: 217–524–9572
Fax: 217–785–6793

Illinois State Police
Computer Crimes Investigation Unit
Master Sgt. James Murray
9511 West Harrison Street
Des Plaines, IL 60016–1562
Phone: 847–294–4549
E-mail: jamurray@leo.gov

Tazewell County State's Attorney CID
Det. Dave Frank
342 Court Street, Suite 6
Pekin, IL 61554–3298
Phone: 309–477–2205, ext. 400
Fax: 309–477–2729
E-mail: sainv@tazewell.com

Indiana

Evansville Police Department
Det. J. Walker/Det. Craig Jordan
Fraud Investigations
15 N.W. Martin Luther King, Jr., Boulevard
Evansville IN, 47708
Phone: 812–436–7995/812–436–7994
E-mail: Jwalker@evansvillepolice.com
        cjordan@evansvillepolice.com

Indiana State Police
Det. David L. Lloyd
Computer Crime Unit
5811 Ellison Road
Fort Wayne, IN 46750
Phone: 219–432–8661
E-mail: ispdet@aol.com

Indianapolis Police Department
Det. William J. Howard
901 North Post Road, Room 115
Indianapolis, IN 46219
Phone: 317–327–3461
E-mail: vulcan@netdirect.net

Iowa

Iowa Division of Criminal Investigation
Doug Elrick
Criminalist
502 East Ninth Street
Des Moines, IA 50319
Phone: 515–281–3666
Fax: 515–281–7638
E-mail: elrick@dps.state.ia.us

Kansas

Kansas Bureau of Investigation
High Technology Crime Investigation
    Unit (HTCIU)
David J. Schroeder
Senior Special Agent
1620 S.W. Tyler Street
Topeka, KS 66612–1837
Phone: 785–296–8222
Fax: 785–296–0525
E-mail: schroeder@kbi.state.ks.us

Olathe Police Department
Sgt. Edward McGillivray
501 East 56 Highway
Olathe, KS 66061
Phone: 913–782–4500
E-mail: emcgillivray@olatheks.org

Wichita Police Department
Forensic Computer Crimes Unit
Det. Shaun Price/Det. Randy Stone
455 North Main, Sixth Floor Lab
Wichita, KS 67202
Phone: 316–268–4102/316–268–4128
E-mail: forensics@kscable.com
    shaun@kscable.com
    rstone@feist.com

Kentucky

Boone County Sheriff
Det. Daren Harris
P.O. Box 198
Burlington, KY 41005
Phone: 859–334–2175
E-mail: dharris@boonecountyky.org

Louisiana

Gonzales Police Department
Officer Victoria Smith
120 South Irma Boulevard
Gonzales, LA 70737
Phone: 225–647–7511
Fax: 225–647–9544
E-mail: vsmith@leo.gov

Louisiana Department of Justice
Criminal Division
High Technology Crime Unit
P.O. Box 94095
Baton Rouge, LA 70804
James L. Piker, Assistant Attorney General
Section Chief, High Technology Crime Unit
Investigator Clayton Rives
Phone: 225–342–7552
Fax: 225–342–7893
E-mail: PikerJ@ag.state.la.us
    RivesCS@ag.state.la.us
Scott Turner, Computer Forensic Examiner
Phone: 225–342–4060
Fax: 225–342–3482
E-mail: TurnerS@ag.state.la.us

Maine

Maine Computer Crimes Task Force
171 Park Street
Lewiston, ME 04240
Det. James C. Rioux
Phone: 207–784–6422, ext. 250
Investigator Mike Webber
Phone: 207–784–6422, ext. 255
Det. Thomas Bureau
Phone: 207–784–6422, ext. 256

Maryland

**Anne Arundel County Police
    Department**
Computer Crimes Unit
Sgt. Terry M. Crowe
41 Community Place
Crownsville, MD 21032
Phone: 410–222–3419
Fax: 410–987–7433
E-mail: terrymcrowe@aol.com

Department of Maryland State Police
Computer Crimes Unit
D/SGT Barry E. Leese
Unit Commander
7155–C Columbia Gateway Drive
Columbia, MD 21046
Phone: 410–290–1620
Fax: 410–290–1831

Montgomery County Police
Computer Crime Unit
Det. Brian Ford
2350 Research Boulevard
Rockville, MD 20850
Phone: 301–840–2599
E-mail: CCU@co.mo.md.us

Massachusetts

Massachusetts Office of the Attorney General
High Tech and Computer Crime Division
John Grossman, Chief
Assistant Attorney General
One Ashburton Place
Boston, MA 02108
Phone: 617–727–2200

Michigan

Michigan Department of Attorney General
High Tech Crime Unit
18050 Deering
Livonia, MI 48152
Phone: 734–525–4151
Fax: 734–525–4372

Oakland County Sheriff's Department
Computer Crimes Unit
Det./Sgt. Joe Duke, CFCE
1201 North Telegraph Road
Pontiac, MI 48341
Phone: 248–858–4942
Fax: 248–858–9565
Pager: 248–580–4047

Minnesota

Ramsey County Sheriff's Department
14 West Kellogg Boulevard
St. Paul, MN 55102
Phone: 651–266–2797
E-mail: mike.oneill@co.ramsey.mn.us

Mississippi

Biloxi Police Department
Investigator Donnie G. Dobbs
170 Porter Avenue
Biloxi, MS 39530
Phone: 228–432–9382
E-mail: mgc2d11@aol.com

Missouri

St. Louis Metropolitan Police Department
High Tech Crimes Unit
Det. Sgt. Robert Muffler
1200 Clark
St. Louis, MO 63103
Phone: 314–444–5441
E-mail: rjmuffler@slmpd.org

Montana

Montana Division of Criminal Investigation
Computer Crime Unit
Jimmy Weg
Agent in Charge
303 North Roberts, Room 367
Helena, MT 59620
Phone: 406–444–6681
E-mail: jweg@state.mt.us

Nebraska

Lincoln Police Department
Investigator Ed Sexton
575 South 10th Street
Lincoln, NE 68508
Phone: 402–441–7587
E-mail: lpd358@cjis.ci.lincoln.ne.us

Nebraska State Patrol
Internet Crimes Against Children Unit
Sgt. Scott Christensen
Coordinator
4411 South 108th Street
Omaha, NE 68137
Phone: 402–595–2410
Fax: 402–697–1409
E-mail: schriste@nsp.state.ne.us

Nevada

City of Reno, Nevada, Police Department
Computer Crimes Unit
455 East Second Street (street address)
Reno, NV 89502
P.O. Box 1900 (mailing address)
Reno, NV 89505
Phone: 775–334–2107
Fax: 775–785–4026

Nevada Attorney General's Office
John Lusak
Senior Computer Forensic Tech
100 North Carson Street
Carson City, NV 89701
Phone: 775–328–2889
E-mail: jlusak@govmail.state.nv.us

New Hampshire

New Hampshire State Police Forensic Laboratory
Computer Crimes Unit
10 Hazen Drive
Concord, NH 03305
Phone: 603–271–0300

New Jersey

New Jersey Division of Criminal Justice
Computer Analysis and Technology Unit (CATU)
James Parolski
Team Leader
25 Market Street
P.O. Box 085
Trenton, NJ 08625–0085
Phone: 609–984–5256/609–984–6500
Pager: 888–819–1292
E-mail: parolskij@dcj.lps.state.nj.us

Ocean County Prosecutor's Office
Special Investigations Unit/Computer Crimes
Investigator Mike Nevil
P.O. Box 2191
Toms River, NJ 08753
Phone: 732–929–2027, ext. 4014
Fax: 732–240–3338
E-mail: mnevil@leo.gov

New Mexico

New Mexico Gaming Control Board
Information Systems Division
Donovan Lieurance
6400 Uptown Boulevard N.E., Suite 100E
Albuquerque, NM 87110
Phone: 505–841–9719
E-mail: dlieurance@nmgcb.org

Twelfth Judicial District Attorney's Office
Investigator Jack Henderson
1000 New York Avenue, Room 301
Alamogordo, NM 88310
Phone: 505–437–1313, ext. 110
E-mail: jack@wazoo.com

New York

Erie County Sheriff's Office
Computer Crime Unit
10 Delaware Avenue
Buffalo, NY 14202
Phone: 716–662–6150
http://www.erie.gov/sheriff/CCU

Nassau County Police Department
Computer Crime Section
Det. Bill Moylan
970 Brush Hollow Road
Westbury, NY 11590
Phone: 516–573–5275

New York Electronic Crimes Task Force
United States Secret Service
ATSAIC Robert Weaver
7 World Trade Center, 10th Floor
New York, NY 11048
Phone: 212–637–4500

New York Police Department
Computer Investigation and Technology
Unit
1 Police Plaza, Room 1110D
New York, NY 10038
Phone: 212–374–4247
Fax: 212–374–4249
E-mail: citu@nypd.org

New York State Attorney General's Office
Internet Bureau
120 Broadway
New York, NY 10271
Phone: 212–416–6344
http://www.oag.state.ny.us

New York State Department of Taxation and Finance
Office of Deputy Inspector General
W.A. Harriman Campus
Building 9, Room 481
Albany, NY 12227
Phone: 518–485–8698
http://www.tax.state.ny.us

New York State Police
Computer Crime Unit
Ronald R. Stevens
Senior Investigator
Forensic Investigation Center
Building 30, State Campus
1220 Washington Avenue
Albany, NY 12226
Phone: 518–457–5712
Fax: 518–402–2773
E-mail: nyspccu@troopers.state.ny.us

Rockland County Sheriff's Department
Computer Crime Task Force
Det. Lt. John J. Gould
55 New Hempstead Road
New City, NY 10956
Phone: 845–708–7860/845–638–5836
Fax: 845–708–7821
E-mail: gouldjo@co.rockland.ny.us

North Carolina

Raleigh Police Department
Investigator Patrick Niemann
110 South McDowell Street
Raleigh, NC 27601
Phone: 919–890–3555
E-mail: niemannp@raleigh-nc.org

North Dakota

North Dakota Bureau of Criminal Investigation
Tim J. Erickson
Special Agent
P.O. Box 1054
Bismarck, ND 58502–1054
Phone: 701–328–5500
E-mail: te409@state.nd.us

Ohio

Hamilton County Ohio Sheriff's Office
Capt. Pat Olvey
Justice Center
1000 Sycamore Street, Room 110
Cincinnati, OH 45202
Phone: 513–946–6689
Fax: 513–721–3581
http://www.hcso.org
(under the Administration Division)

Ohio Attorney General's Office
Bureau of Criminal Investigation
Computer Crime Unit
Kathleen Barch
Deputy Director
1560 State Route 56
London, OH 43140
Phone: 740–845–2410
E-mail: Kbarch@ag.state.oh.us

Riverside Police Department
Officer Harold Jones
MCSE/Computer Crime Specialist
1791 Harshman Road
Riverside, OH 45424
Phone: 937–904–1425
E-mail: hjones@cops.org

Oklahoma

Oklahoma Attorney General
4545 North Lincoln Boulevard
Suite 260
Oklahoma City, OK 73105–3498
Phone: 405–521–4274
E-mail: jim_powell@oag.state.ok.us

Oklahoma State Bureau of Investigation
Mark R. McCoy, Ed.D., CFCE
Special Agent
P.O. Box 968
Stillwater, OK 74076
Phone: 405–742–8329
Fax: 405–742–8284
E-mail: mmccoy@sprynet.com
      markm@osbi.state.ok.us

Oregon

Portland Police Bureau
Computer Crimes Detail
Det./Sgt. Tom Nelson
Computer Forensic Investigator
1115 S.W. Second Avenue
Portland, OR 97204
Phone: 503–823–0871
E-mail: tnelson@police.ci.portland.or.us

Washington County Sheriff's Office
Brian Budlong
215 S.W. Adams Avenue, MS32
Hillsboro, OR 97123
Phone: 503–846–2573
Fax: 503–846–2637
E-mail: brian_budlong@
    co.washington.or.us

Pennsylvania

Allegheny County Police Department
High Tech Crime Unit
Det. T. Haney
400 North Lexington Street
Pittsburgh, PA 15208
Phone: 412–473–1304
Fax: 412–473–1377
E-mail: thaney@county.allegheny.pa.us

Erie County District Attorney's Office
Erie County Courthouse
140 West Sixth Street
Erie, PA 16501
Phone: 814–451–6349
Fax: 814–451–6419

Rhode Island

Warwick Police Department
BCI Unit, Detective Division
Edmund Pierce
BCI Detective
99 Veterans Memorial Drive
Warwick, RI 02886
Phone: 401–468–4200 (main)/
    401–468–4243 (direct)
E-mail: WPDDetectives@warwickri.com
    efp31@home.com

South Carolina

South Carolina Law Enforcement Division (SLED)
Lt. L.J. "Chip" Johnson
Supervisory Special Agent
P.O. Box 21398
Columbia, SC 29221–1398
Phone: 803–737–9000

Winthrop University
Department of Public Safety
Daniel R. Yeargin
Assistant Chief of Police
02 Crawford Building
Rock Hill, SC 29733
Phone: 803–323–3496
E-mail: yeargind@winthrop.edu

South Dakota

Information unavailable.

Tennessee

Harriman Police Department
Sgt. Brian Farmer
130 Pansy Hill Road
Harriman, TN 37748
Phone: 865–882–3383
Fax: 865–882–0700
E-mail: crimeseen@earthlink.net
        bsfarmer@bellsouth.net

Knox County Sheriff's Office
Carleton Bryant
Staff Attorney
400 West Main Avenue
Knoxville, TN 37902
Phone: 865–971–3911
E-mail: sheriff@esper.com

Tennessee Attorney General's Office
Susan Holmes
Forensic Technology Specialist
425 Fifth Avenue, North
Nashville, TN 37243
Phone: 615–532–9658
E-mail: sholmes@mail.state.tn.us

Texas

Austin Police Department
715 East Eighth Street
Austin, TX 78701
http://www.ci.austin.tx.us/police

Bexar County District Attorney's Office
Russ Brandau/David Getrost
300 Dolorosa
San Antonio, TX 78205
Phone: 210–335–2974/210–335–2991
E-mail: rbrandau@co.bexar.tx.us
        dgetrost@co.bexar.tx.us

Dallas Police Department
2014 Main Street
Dallas, TX 75201
http://www.ci.dallas.tx.us/dpd

**Federal Bureau of Investigation
Dallas Field Office**
1801 North Lamar Street
Dallas, TX 75202–1795
Phone: 214–720–2200
http://www.fbi.gov/contact/fo/dl/dallas.htm

Houston Police Department
1200 Travis Street
Houston, TX 77002
http://www.ci.houston.tx.us/departme/police

Portland Police Department
Det. Terrell Elliott
902 Moore Avenue
Portland, TX 78374
Phone: 361–643–2546
Fax: 361–643–5689
E-mail: telliott@portlandpd.com
http://www.portlandpd.com

Texas Department of Public Safety
5805 North Lamar Boulevard (street
    address)
Austin, TX 78752–4422
P.O. Box 4087 (mailing address)
Austin, TX 78773–0001
Phone: 512–424–2200/800–252–5402
E-mail: specialcrimes@txdps.state.tx.us
http://www.txdps.state.tx.us

Utah

Utah Department of Public Safety
Criminal Investigations Bureau, Forensic
    Computer Lab
Daniel D. Hooper
Special Agent
5272 South College Drive, Suite 200
Murray, UT 84123
Phone: 801–284–6238
E-mail: dhooper@dps.state.ut.us

Vermont

Internet Crimes Task Force
Det. Sgt. Michael Schirling
50 Cherry Street, Suite 102
Burlington, VT 05401
Phone: 802–652–6800/802–652–6899
E-mail: mschirli@dps.state.vt.us

**State of Vermont Department of
    Public Safety**
Bureau of Criminal Investigation
Sgt. Mark Lauer
103 South Main Street
Waterbury, VT 05671–2101
Phone: 802–241–5367
Fax: 802–241–5349
E-mail: mlauer@dps.state.vt.us

Virginia

Arlington County Police Department
Criminal Investigations Division
Computer Forensics
Det. Ray Rimer
1425 North Courthouse Road
Arlington, VA 22201
Phone: 703–228–4239
Pager: 703–866–8965
E-mail: rimer550@erols.com

Fairfax County Police Department
Computer Forensics Section
Lt. Doug Crooke
4100 Chain Bridge Road
Fairfax, VA 22030
Phone: 703–246–7800
Fax: 703–246–4253
E-mail: douglas.crooke@co.fairfax.va.us
http://www.co.fairfax.va.us/ps/police/
    homepage.htm

Richmond Police Department
Technology Crimes Section
Det. Jeff Deem
501 North Ninth Street
Richmond, VA 23219
Phone: 804–646–3949
Pager: 804–783–3021
E-mail: jdeem@ci.richmond.va.us

Virginia Beach Police Department
Det. Michael Encarnacao
Special Investigations CERU
2509 Princess Anne Road
Virginia Beach, VA 23456
Phone: 757–427–1749
E-mail: mikee@cops.org

Virginia Department of Motor Vehicles
Law Enforcement Section
Larry L. Barnett
Assistant Special Agent in Charge
945 Edwards Ferry Road
Leesburg, VA 20175
Phone: 703–771–4757
E-mail: lbtrip@erols.com

Virginia Office of the Attorney General
Addison L. Cheeseman
Senior Criminal Investigator
900 East Main Street
Richmond, VA 23219
Phone: 804–786–6554
E-mail: acheeseman@oag.state.va.us

Virginia State Police
Andrew Clark, CFCE
Computer Technology Specialist 3
Richmond, VA 23236
Phone: 804–323–2040
E-mail: AndyClark@att.net

Washington

King County Sheriff's Office
Fraud/Computer Forensic Unit
Sgt. Steve Davis/Det. Brian Palmer
401 Fourth Avenue North, RJC 104
Kent, WA 98032–4429
Phone: 206–296–4280
E-mail: steven.davis@metrokc.gov
　　　　bk.palmer@metrokc.gov

Lynnwood Police Department
High Tech Property Crimes
Det. Douglas J. Teachworth
19321 44th Avenue West (street address)
P.O. Box 5008 (mailing address)
Lynnwood, WA 98046–5008
Phone: 425–744–6916
E-mail: dteachworth@ci.lynnwood.wa.us

Tacoma Police Department
PCSO
Det. Richard Voce
930 Tacoma Avenue South
Tacoma, WA 98402
Phone: 253–591–5679
E-mail: rvoce@ci.tacoma.wa.us

Vancouver Police Department
Maggi Holbrook
Computer Forensics Specialist
300 East 13th Street
Vancouver, WA 98660
Phone: 360–735–8887
E-mail: ecrimes@ci.vancouver.wa.us

Washington State Department of Fish and Wildlife
John D. Flanagan, ITAS3
600 Capitol Way North
Olympia, WA 98501
Phone: 360–902–2210
Cell phone: 360–349–1225
E-mail: flanajdf@dfw.wa.gov

Washington State Patrol
Computer Forensics Unit
Det./Sgt. Steve Beltz
Airdustrial Way, Building 17
Olympia, WA 98507–2347
Phone: 360–753–3277
E-mail: sbeltz505@aol.com
　　　　sbeltz@wsp.wa.gov

West Virginia

National White Collar Crime Center
1000 Technology Drive, Suite 2130
Fairmont, WV 26554
Phone: 877–628–7674
http://www.cybercrime.org

Wisconsin

Green Bay Police Department
Specialist Rick Dekker
307 South Adams Street
Green Bay, WI 54301
E-mail: rickdk@ci.green-bay.wi.us

Wisconsin Department of Justice
P.O. Box 7857
Madison, WI 53707–7851
Phone: 608–266–1221
http://www.doj.state.wi.us

Wood County Sheriff's Department
400 Market Street
Wis Rapids, WI 54495
Phone: 715–421–8700
E-mail: wcsd@tznet.com

Wyoming

Casper Police Department
Det. Derrick Dietz
210 North David
Casper, WY 82601
Phone: 307–235–8489
E-mail: ddietz@cityofcasperwy.com

Gillette Police Department
Sgt. Dave Adsit
201 East Fifth Street
Gillette, WY 82716
Phone: 307–682–5109
E-mail: davea@www.ci.gillette.wy.us

Green River Police Department
Corp. Tom Jarvie/Sgt. David Hyer
50 East Second North
Green River, WY 82935
Phone: 307–872–0555
E-mail: tjarvie@cityofgreenriver.org
         dhyer@cityofgreenriver.org

**Wyoming Division of Criminal
   Investigation**
316 West 22nd Street
Cheyenne, WY 82002
Phone: 307–777–7183
Fax: 307–777–7252
Stephen J. Miller, Special Agent
E-mail: smille2@state.wy.us
Patrick Seals, Special Agent
E-mail: pseals@state.wy.us
Michael B. Curran, Special Agent
E-mail: mcurra@state.wy.us
Flint Waters, Special Agent
E-mail: fwater@state.wy.us

International

Australia

Western Australia Police
Det./Sgt. Ted Wisniewski
Computer Crime Investigation
Commercial Crime Division
Level 7 Eastpoint Plaza
233 Adelaide Tce
Perth WA 6000
Phone: +61 8 92200700
Fax: +61 8 92254489
E-mail: Computer.Crime@
       police.wa.gov.au

Brazil

**Instituto De Criminalística - Polícia
Civil Do Distrito Federal**
SAISO - Lote 23 - Bloco "C" Complexo
   de Poilcia Civil
70610–200
Brasília, Brazil
Phone: 55 +61 362–5948/55 +61
   233–9530
E-mail: perint@pcdf.df.gov.br

Canada

Royal Canadian Mounted Police
Technical Operations Directorate
Technological Crime Branch
1426 St. Joseph Boulevard
Gloucester, Ontario
Canada
KIA OR2
Phone: 613–993–1777

Switzerland

Computer Crime Unit (GCI)
Det. Pascal Seeger/Det. Didiser Frezza
5, ch. de la Graviere
1227 Acacias, Geneva
Switzerland
Phone: +41 22 427.80.16 (17)
Fax: +41 22 820.30.16
E-mail: gci@police.ge.ch

United Kingdom

HM Inland Revenue
Special Compliance Office
Forensic Computing Team
Barkley House
P.O. Box 20
Castle Meadow Road
Nottingham
NG2 1BA
UK
Phone: +44 (0)115 974 0887
Fax: +44 (0)115 974 0890
E-mail: lindsay.j.scrimshaw@ir.gsi.gov.uk

National High-Tech Crime Unit
P.O. Box 10101
London
E14 9NF
UK
Phone: +44 (0) 870–241–0549
Fax: +44 (0) 870–241–5729
E-mail: admin@nhtcu.org

Training Resources List

Canadian Police College
P.O. Box 8900
Ottawa, Ontario
K1G 3J2
Canada
Phone: 613–993–9500
E-mail: cpc@cpc.gc.ca
http://www.cpc.gc.ca

DoD Computer Investigations Training Program
911 Elkridge Landing Road
Airport Square 11 Building
Suite 200
Linthicum, MD 21090
Phone: 410–981–1604
Fax: 410–850–8906
E-mail: info@dcitp.gov
http://www.dcitp.gov

FBI Academy at Quantico
U.S. Marine Corps Base
Quantico, VA
Phone: 703–640–6131
http://www.fbi.gov/programs/
academy/academy.htm

Federal Law Enforcement Training Center
Headquarters Facility
Glynco, GA 31524
Phone: 912–267–2100
http://www.fletc.gov

Federal Law Enforcement Training Center
Artesia Facility
1300 West Richey Avenue
Artesia, NM 88210
Phone: 505–748–8000
http://www.fletc.gov

Federal Law Enforcement Training Center
Charleston Facility
2000 Bainbridge Avenue
Charleston, SC 29405–2607
Phone: 843–743–8858
http://www.fletc.gov

Florida Association of Computer Crime Investigators, Inc.
P.O. Box 1503
Bartow, FL 33831–1503
Phone: 352–357–0500
E-mail: info@facci.org
http://www.facci.org

Forensic Association of Computer Technologists
Doug Elrick
P.O. Box 703
Des Moines, IA 50303
Phone: 515–281–7671
http://www.byteoutofcrime.org

High Technology Crime Investigation Association (International)
1474 Freeman Drive
Amissville, VA 20106
Phone: 540–937–5019
http://www.htcia.org

Information Security University
149 New Montgomery Street
Second Floor
San Francisco, CA 94105
http://www.infosecu.com

Information Systems Security Association (ISSA)
7044 South 13th Street
Oak Creek, WI 53154
Phone: 800–370–4772
http://www.issa.org

Institute of Police Technology and Management
University of North Florida
12000 Alumni Drive
Jacksonville, FL 32224–2678
Phone: 904–620–4786
Fax: 904–620–2453
http://www.iptm.org

International Association of Computer Investigative Specialists (IACIS)
P.O. Box 21688
Keizer, OR 97307–1688
Phone: 503–557–1506
E-mail: admin@cops.org
http://www.cops.org

International Organization on Computer Evidence
Phone: +44 (0) 171–230–6485
E-mail: lwr@fss.org.uk
http://www.ioce.org

James Madison University
800 South Main Street
Harrisonburg, VA 22807
Phone: 540–568–6211
http://www.cs.jmu.edu/currentcourses.htm

Midwest Electronic Crime Investigators Association
http://www.mecia.org

National Center for Forensic Science
University of Central Florida
P.O. Box 162367
Orlando, FL 32816–2367
Phone: 407–823–6469
E-mail: natlctr@mail.ucf.edu
http://www.ncfs.ucf.edu

National Colloquium for Information Systems Security Education (NCISSE)
http://www.ncisse.org

National Criminal Justice Computer Laboratory and Training Center SEARCH Group, Inc.
7311 Greenhaven Drive, Suite 145
Sacramento, CA 95831
Phone: 916–392–2550
http://www.search.org

National Cybercrime Training Partnership (NCTP)
1000 Technology Drive, Suite 2130
Fairmont, WV 26554
Phone: 877–628–7674
E-mail: info@nctp.org
http://www.nctp.org
Note: New CD-ROM available, *Prosecuting Cases That Involve Computers: A Resource for State and Local Prosecutors*

National White Collar Crime Center
1000 Technology Drive, Suite 2130
Fairmont, WV 26554
Phone: 877–628–7674
http://www.cybercrime.org
Note: New CD-ROM available, *Prosecuting Cases That Involve Computers: A Resource for State and Local Prosecutors*

New Technologies, Inc.
2075 N.E. Division Street
Gresham, OR 97030
Phone: 503–661–6912
E-mail: info@forensics-intl.com
http://www.forensics-intl.com

Purdue University
CERIAS (Center for Education and
Research in Information and
Assurance Security)
Andra C. Short
Recitation Building
Purdue University
West Lafayette, IN 47907–1315
Phone: 765–494–7806
E-mail: acs@cerias.purdue.edu
http://www.cerias.purdue.edu

Redlands Community College
Clayton Hoskinson, CFCE
Program Coordinator
Criminal Justice and Forensic
Computer Science
1300 South Country Club Road
El Reno, OK 73036–5304
Phone: 405–262–2552, ext. 2517
E-mail: hoskinsonc@redlandscc.net

University of New Haven
School of Public Safety and
Professional Studies
300 Orange Avenue
West Haven, CT 06516
http://www.newhaven.edu

**University of New Haven–California
Campus**
Forensic Computer Investigation Program
6060 Sunrise Vista Drive
Citrus Heights, CA 95610
http://www.newhaven.edu

U.S. Department of Justice
Criminal Division
Computer Crime and Intellectual Property
Section (CCIPS)
1301 New York Avenue N.W.
Washington, DC 20530
Phone: 202–514–1026
http://www.cycbercrime.gov

Utica College
Economic Crime Programs
1600 Burrstone Road
Utica, NY 13502
http://www.ecii.edu

**Wisconsin Association of Computer
Crime Investigators**
P.O. Box 510212
New Berlin, WI 53151–0212
http://www.wacci.org

References

Anonymous. *Maximum Security: A Hacker's Guide to Protecting Your Internet Site and Network, Second Edition.* Indianapolis, Indiana: Sams, 1998.

Blacharski, Dan. *Network Security in a Mixed Environment.* Foster City, California: IDG Books, 1998.

Casey, Eoghan. *Digital Evidence and Computer Crime: Forensic Science, Computers and the Internet.* San Diego: Academic Press, 2000.

Cheswick, William R. and Steven M. Bellovin. *Firewalls and Internet Security: Repelling the Wily Hacker.* Boston, Massachusetts: Addison-Wesley, 1994.

Cohen, Frederick B. *A Short Course on Computer Viruses.* Somerset, New Jersey: John Wiley & Sons, 1994.

Davis, William S. *Computing Fundamentals: Concepts, Third Edition.* Boston, Massachusetts: Addison-Wesley Publishing Co., 1991.

Deffie, Whitfield and Susan Landau. *Privacy on the Line: The Politics of Wiretapping and Encryption.* Cambridge, Massachusetts: MIT Press, 1998.

Deloitte, Haskins & Sells. *Computer Viruses: Proceedings of an Invitational Symposium, October 10–11, 1988.* New York: Deloitte, Haskins & Sells, 1989.

Denning, Dorothy E. *Information Warfare and Security.* Boston, Massachusetts: Addison-Wesley, 1999.

Denning, D. and P. Denning. *Internet Besieged: Countering Cyberspace Scofflaws.* New York: Addison-Wesley, 1997.

Fiery, Dennis. *Secrets of a Super Hacker.* Port Townsend, Washington: Loompanics Unlimited, 1994.

Ford, Merilee, H. Kim Lew, Steve Spanier, and Tim Stevenson. *Internetworking Technologies Handbook.* Indianapolis, Indiana: New Riders Publishing, 1997.

Garfinkel, Simson and Gene Spafford. *Practical UNIX & Internet Security, Second Edition.* Sebastopol, California: O'Reilly & Associates, Inc., 1996.

Garfinkel, Simson and Gene Spafford. *Web Security & Commerce.* Sebastopol, California: O'Reilly & Associates, Inc., 1997.

Guisnel, Jean. *Cyberwars: Espionage on the Internet.* New York: Plenum Press, 1997.

Hafner, Katie and John Markoff. *Cyberpunk.* New York: Simon & Schuster, Inc., 1995.

Landreth, Bill. *Out of the Inner Circle.* Redmond, Washington: Tempus Books of Microsoft Press, 1989.

Levin, Richard B. *The Computer Virus Handbook.* Berkeley, California: Osborne/McGraw-Hill, 1990.

Ludwig, Mark. *The Giant Black Book of Computer Viruses, Second Edition.* Show Low, Arizona: American Eagle Publications, Inc., 1998.

Martin, Fredrick T. *Top Secret Intranet.* Old Tappan, New Jersey: Prentice Hall PTR, 1998.

McCarthy, Linda. *Intranet Security.* Palo Alto, California: Sun Microsystems Press, 1998.

McClure, Stuart, Joel Scambray, and George Kurtz. *Hacking Exposed.* Berkeley, California: Osborne/McGraw-Hill, 1999.

Meinel, Carolyn P. *The Happy Hacker, Second Edition.* Show Low, Arizona: American Eagle Publications, Inc., 1998.

National Institute of Justice. *Crime Scene Investigation: A Guide for Law Enforcement.* Washington, D.C.: U.S. Department of Justice, National Institute of Justice, 2000. NCJ 178280.

National Research Council. *Computers at Risk: Safe Computing in the Information Age.* Washington, D.C.: National Academy Press, 1991.

National White Collar Crime Center. *Using the Internet as an Investigative Tool, First Edition.* Fairmont, West Virginia: National White Collar Crime Center, 1999.

Northcutt, Stephen. *Network Intrusion Detection: An Analyst's Handbook.* Indianapolis, Indiana: New Riders Publishing, 1999.

Olson-Raymer, Gayle. Terrorism: *A Historical & Contemporary Perspective.* New York: American Heritage Custom Publishing, 1996.

Parker, Donn B. *Fighting Computer Crime.* New York: Scribners, 1983.

Parker, Donn B. *Fighting Computer Crime: A New Framework for Protecting Information.* New York: John Wiley & Sons, Inc., 1998.

Parsaye, Kamran and Mark Chignell. *Expert Systems for Experts.* New York: John Wiley & Sons, Inc., 1988.

Pipkin, Donald L. *Halting the Hacker: A Practical Guide to Computer Security.* Upper Saddle River, New Jersey: Prentice Hall, 1997.

Raymond, Eric S. *The New Hacker's Dictionary, Third Edition.* London, England: MIT Press, 1998.

Robbins, Arnold. *UNIX in a Nutshell, Third Edition.* Sebastopol, California: O'Reilly and Associates, Inc., 1999.

Rodgers, Ulka. *ORACLE: A Database Developer's Guide.* Upper Saddle River, New Jersey: Yourdon Press, 1991.

Rosenblatt, Kenneth S. *High-Technology Crime: Investigating Cases Involving Computers.* San Jose, California: KSK Publications, 1996.

Rosenoer, Jonathan. *CyberLaw: The Law of the Internet.* New York: Springer, 1997.

Russell, Deborah and G.T. Gangemi, Sr. *Computer Security Basics.* Sebastopol, California: O'Reilly & Associates, Inc., 1992.

Schulman, Mark. *Introduction to UNIX.* Indianapolis, Indiana: Que Corporation, 1992.

Schwartau, Winn. *Information Warfare: Chaos on the Electronic Superhighway.* New York: Thunder's Mouth Press, 1995.

Shimomura, Tsutomu and John Markoff. *Take-Down.* New York: Hyperion, 1996.

Slatalla, Michelle and Joshua Quittner. *The Gang That Ruled Cyberspace.* New York: Harper Collins, 1995.

Sterling, Bruce. *The Hacker Crackdown.* New York: Bantam Books, 1993.

Stoll, Cliff. *The Cuckoo's Egg.* New York: Simon & Schuster, Inc., 1989.

Strassmann, Paul A. *The Politics of Information Management Policy Guidelines.* New Canaan, Connecticut: The Information Economic Press, 1995.

Tittel, Ed and Margaret Robbins. *Network Design Essentials.* Boston, Massachusetts: Academic Press, Inc., 1994.

Trippi, Robert R., and Efraim Turban. *Neural Networks in Finance and Investing.* Cambridge, England: Probus Publishing Co., 1993.

U.S. Department of Justice, Computer Crime and Intellectual Property Section. *Searching and Seizing Computers and Obtaining Electronic Evidence in Criminal Investigations.* Washington, D.C.: U.S. Department of Justice, Computer Crime and Intellectual Property Section, 2001.

Wang, Wallace. *Steal This Computer Book.* San Francisco, California: No Starch Press, 1998.

Wolff, Michael. *How You Can Access the Facts and Cover Your Tracks Using the Internet and Online Services.* New York: Wolff New Media, LLC, 1996.

List of Organizations

The following is a list of organizations to which a draft copy of this document was mailed.

Alaska Criminal Laboratory

American Academy of Forensic Sciences

American Bar Association

American Society of Law Enforcement Trainers

Anchorage, Alaska, Police Department

Arapahoe County, Colorado, Sheriff's Office

Association of Federal Defense Attorneys

Bridgeport, Michigan, Forensic Laboratory

Bureau of Justice Assistance

Canadian Police Research Center

Cleveland State College Basic Police Academy

Commission of Accreditation for Law Enforcement Agencies

Connecticut Department of Public Safety

Council of State Governments

Crime Scene Academy

Criminal Justice Institute

Dallas County District Attorney

Fairbanks, Alaska, Police Department

Federal Bureau of Investigation

Federal Law Enforcement Training Center

Florida Department of Law Enforcement

Florida Department of Law Enforcement-Jacksonville Regional Operations Center

Florida Office of Statewide Prosecution

Frederick County, Maryland, State's Attorney's Office

Georgia Bureau of Investigation

Harlingen, Texas, Police Department

High Tech Crime Consortium

Illinois State Police

Indiana State Police Laboratory

Institute for Intergovernmental Research

Institute of Police Technology and Management

Internal Revenue Service, Criminal Investigations

International Association of Bomb Technicians and Investigators

International Association of Chiefs of Police

International Association for Identification

Juneau, Alaska, Police Department

LaGrange, Georgia, Police Department

Law Enforcement Training Institute

Maine State Police Crime Laboratory

Massachusetts State Police Crime Laboratory

Metro Nashville Police Academy

Metro Nashville Police Department

Middletown Township, New Jersey, Police Department

National Advocacy Center

National Association of Attorneys General

National District Attorneys Association

National Law Enforcement and Corrections Technology Center–Northeast

National Law Enforcement and Corrections Technology Center–Rocky Mountain

National Law Enforcement and Corrections Technology Center–Southeast

National Law Enforcement Council

National Sheriffs' Association

National White Collar Crime Center

Naval Criminal Investigative Service

New Hampshire State Police Forensic Laboratory

New York Police Department

North Carolina Justice Academy

Office of the District Attorney General-Nashville, Tennessee

Office of Law Enforcement Technology Commercialization

Office of Overseas Prosecutorial Development

Ohio Bureau of Criminal ID and Investigation

Orange County, California, Community College–Department of Criminal Justice

Orange County Sheriff's Department–Forensic Science Services

Peace Officers Standards and Training

Pharr, Texas, Police Department

Regional Computer Forensic Laboratory

Rhode Island State Crime Laboratory

Sedgwick County, Kansas, District Attorney's Office

Sitka, Alaska, Police Department

Social Security Administration–Office of the Inspector General

State of Florida Crime Laboratory

TASC, Inc.

Tennessee Bureau of Investigation

Tennessee Law Enforcement Training Academy

Texas Rangers Department of Public Safety

Town of Goshen, New York, Police Department

U.S. Army Criminal Investigation Laboratory

U.S. Attorney's Office–Western District of New York

U.S. Customs Service Cybersmuggling Center

U.S. Department of Justice–Criminal Division

U.S. Department of Justice–Fraud Section

U.S. Department of Justice–Office of Overseas Prosecutorial Development

U.S. Department of Justice–Western District of Michigan

U.S. Postal Service–Office of Inspector General

Virginia State Police Academy

About the National Institute of Justice

NIJ is the research and development agency of the U.S. Department of Justice and is the only Federal agency solely dedicated to researching crime control and justice issues. NIJ provides objective, independent, nonpartisan, evidence-based knowledge and tools to meet the challenges of crime and justice, particularly at the State and local levels. NIJ's principal authorities are derived from the Omnibus Crime Control and Safe Streets Act of 1968, as amended (42 U.S.C. §§ 3721–3722).

NIJ's Mission

In partnership with others, NIJ's mission is to prevent and reduce crime, improve law enforcement and the administration of justice, and promote public safety. By applying the disciplines of the social and physical sciences, NIJ—

- **Researches** the nature and impact of crime and delinquency.
- **Develops** applied technologies, standards, and tools for criminal justice practitioners.
- **Evaluates** existing programs and responses to crime.
- **Tests** innovative concepts and program models in the field.
- **Assists** policymakers, program partners, and justice agencies.
- **Disseminates** knowledge to many audiences.

NIJ's Strategic Direction and Program Areas

NIJ is committed to five challenges as part of its strategic plan: 1) **rethinking justice** and the processes that create just communities; 2) **understanding the nexus** between social conditions and crime; 3) **breaking the cycle** of crime by testing research-based interventions; 4) **creating the tools** and technologies that meet the needs of practitioners; and 5) **expanding horizons** through interdisciplinary and international perspectives. In addressing these strategic challenges, the Institute is involved in the following program areas: crime control and prevention, drugs and crime, justice systems and offender behavior, violence and victimization, communications and information technologies, critical incident response, investigative and forensic sciences (including DNA), less-than-lethal technologies, officer protection, education and training technologies, testing and standards, technology assistance to law enforcement and corrections agencies, field testing of promising programs, and international crime control. NIJ communicates its findings through conferences and print and electronic media.

NIJ's Structure

The NIJ Director is appointed by the President and confirmed by the Senate. The NIJ Director establishes the Institute's objectives, guided by the priorities of the Office of Justice Programs, the U.S. Department of Justice, and the needs of the field. NIJ actively solicits the views of criminal justice and other professionals and researchers to inform its search for the knowledge and tools to guide policy and practice.

NIJ has three operating units. The Office of Research and Evaluation manages social science research and evaluation and crime mapping research. The Office of Science and Technology manages technology research and development, standards development, and technology assistance to State and local law enforcement and corrections agencies. The Office of Development and Communications manages field tests of model programs, international research, and knowledge dissemination programs. NIJ is a component of the Office of Justice Programs, which also includes the Bureau of Justice Assistance, the Bureau of Justice Statistics, the Office of Juvenile Justice and Delinquency Prevention, and the Office for Victims of Crime.

To find out more about the National Institute of Justice, please contact:

National Criminal Justice Reference Service
P.O. Box 6000
Rockville, MD 20849–6000
800–851–3420
e-mail: *askncjrs@ncjrs.org*

To obtain an electronic version of this document, access the NIJ Web site
(*http://www.ojp.usdoj.gov/nij*).